THE HISTORY OF
AIR FORCES
AROUND THE WORLD

THE HISTORY OF
AIR FORCES
AROUND THE WORLD

EDITED BY SHALINI SAXENA
SUPPLEMENTAL MATERIAL BY MICHAEL RAY

Britannica
Educational Publishing
IN ASSOCIATION WITH

ROSEN
EDUCATIONAL SERVICES

Published in 2014 by Britannica Educational Publishing (a trademark of Encyclopædia Britannica, Inc.) in association with The Rosen Publishing Group, Inc.
29 East 21st Street, New York, NY 10010

Distributed exclusively by Rosen Publishing.
To see additional Britannica Educational Publishing titles, go to rosenpublishing.com.

First Edition

Britannica Educational Publishing
J.E. Luebering: Director, Core Reference Group
Anthony L. Green: Editor, Compton's by Britannica

Rosen Publishing
Hope Lourie Killcoyne: Executive Editor
Shalini Saxena: Editor
Nelson Sá: Art Director
Brian Garvey: Designer
Cindy Reiman: Photography Manager

Library of Congress Cataloging-in-Publication Data

The history of air forces around the world/Shalini Saxena ; introduction and supplementary material by Michael Ray.—First edition.
     pages cm..—(The world's armed forces)
Includes bibliographical references and index.
ISBN 978-1-62275-145-7 (library bound)
1. Air forces.—History.—Juvenile literature. 2. United States. Air Force.—History.—Juvenile literature. I. Saxena, Shalini, 1982– editor.
UG630.H59 2013
358.4009.—dc23

                                                                2013035358

Manufactured in the United States of America

On the cover: *(Top)* An F-117 Nighthawk stealth vehicle of the United States Air Force. © *iStockphoto. com/Dan Prat.. (Bottom left)* A captain in the 40th Expeditionary Bomb Squadron of the United States Air Force piloting a B-52 bomber after a mission during the Iraq War. *USAF/Getty Images. (Bottom right)* Members of the People's Liberation Army Air Force of China marching in stride during a rehearsal drill before a parade in Beijing. *Feng Li/Getty Images.*

Cover and interior pages *(camouflage pattern)* © *iStockphoto.com/EvgeniyDzhulay*

CONTENTS

An early balloon used for reconnaissance during the Civil War. Library of Congress Prints and Photographs Division

INTRODUCTION

Commanders had long recognized the advantage that could be gained from controlling the skies over a battlefield. However, it was not until the time of the French Revolutionary Wars and the American Civil War that they could realistically achieve that advantage. Those conflicts saw the first uses of observation balloons to monitor an enemy's movements. The inability to reliably steer balloons, their vulnerability to enemy fire from the ground, and their lack of offensive weaponry made balloons more of a novelty than a direct threat to opposing troops. Nonetheless, the skies had been militarized, and the 20th century would see radical changes in military doctrine to accommodate this new frontier in warfare and defense. This book will profile the technologies and tactics that have led to the growth and evolution of air forces from the earliest lighter-than-air craft to the unmanned aerial vehicles of the 21st-century battlespace.

One of the core concepts of military science is force projection. Force projection is the ability of a country's military to conduct operations outside that country's established borders. The greater a country's force projection capability, the greater its influence—both politically and militarily around—the world. Early armies exercised force projection by maintaining frontier garrisons or patrolling roads that were frequently used by merchants or pilgrims. The British navy maintained control of the world's sea lanes as a measure of force projection during the era of the British Empire (it retains some measure of that control to this day through Britain's overseas territories).

The expansion of air power revolutionized the way in which countries could project force. The Japanese attack on Pearl Harbor in 1941 demonstrated that naval air power could be used in a devastating manner to strike targets thousands of miles away. The Berlin airlift, which utilized air transport to bring relief to the blockaded city of West Berlin in 1948–49, was a classic demonstration of "soft power" projection. The development of strategic weapons systems such as long-range bombers and innovations such as in-air refueling greatly expanded the sphere of action for air forces, and targets on the other side of the world were suddenly within reach.

The launch of the Soviet spacecraft *Sputnik* in 1957 inaugurated the satellite age and ignited the Space Race, as the United States and the Soviet Union sought to assert control of the "final frontier." The *Apollo* astronauts went to the Moon, and private companies joined national governments in the orbital skies, as telecommunications satellites transformed the way in which information was transmitted around the world. The Navstar Global Positioning System (GPS), a constellation of satellites originally used by the United States Department of Defense for military purposes, has fundamentally changed the way in which humans navigate the world around them. Recognizing the "soft power" implications of a single country controlling such a powerful tool, Russia, China, and the European Union have all embarked on similar programs. Whether through "soft power" or "hard power," air forces provide modern military planners with a range of options—and challenges—undreamed of by those early balloonists.

WHAT IS AN AIR FORCE?

CHAPTER 1

This is an age of air power, and the military strength of a nation depends in great part upon the effectiveness of its air force. All of the major countries of the world maintain air forces as part of their defense systems. Air power also reaches into outer space, where satellites control modern weapons and communications systems.

The contemporary air force relies on computer and radar technology to control fleets of fighters, bombers, transports, and reconnaissance (spy) craft. Modern airplanes can carry missiles and bombs, as well as machine guns, while tanker planes can refuel fighters and bombers in the air to lengthen flight time.

ORGANIZATION

Most of the world's air forces organize their resources in similar ways. Air forces either are dependent units of an army, navy, or unified defense system or are autonomous service branches.

Four generations of fighter craft of the United States Air Force flying over Hampton Roads, Va., in a Heritage Flight during an air show.
U.S. Air Force/Getty Images

Air force members hold military ranks similar to those of other services. Commissioned officers are usually headed by generals, as in France, or by marshals, as in Great Britain. These are followed by some mix of commodores, colonels, group captains, lieutenant colonels, commanders, wing and squadron leaders, lieutenants, and pilot officers. Enlisted men and women generally include sergeants, corporals, privates, and aircraftsmen.

In many nations the smallest units of planes and personnel are called flights. These traditionally consist of three or four aircraft. Larger organizational units include squadrons, wings, divisions, and commands. The major combat commands of the United States Air Force, for example, are each organized into at least two divisions. They, in turn, contain wings of dozens of planes. Wings are further divided into squadrons composed of several flights of aircraft.

Air force commands usually perform one of five military functions: strategic, tactical, air defense, logistical, or training. Often the duties of a command change in response to new national and international needs and improved weapons.

Strategic commands involve attack and bombing missions. They rely on the use of heavy bombers as well as strategic missile systems. These systems include intercontinental ballistic missiles, which are equipped with nuclear warheads and are launched from underground silos, and air-to-surface attack missiles, which are launched from aircraft onto enemy defenses. In some countries, such as the United States and Japan, the strategic command also uses space satellites

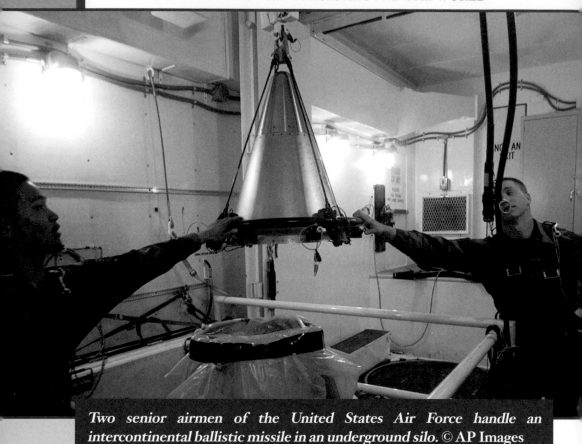

Two senior airmen of the United States Air Force handle an intercontinental ballistic missile in an underground silo. © AP Images

for such activities as surveillance and recon- naissance. In the early 21st century, remotely piloted unmanned aerial vehicles (UAVs) were an increasingly important tool for strategic commands, providing real-time battlefield intelligence and acting as precision weapons platforms that could loiter over a target for up to 24 hours.

Tactical commands are responsible for fighting enemy aircraft and for providing air support to ground troops. These commands rely on fighter and fighter-bomber aircraft for their operations. Tactical planes can be armed with guns, rockets, nuclear bombs, and guided missiles.

Air defense commands protect the airspace of a nation and provide reconnaissance systems to monitor enemy attacks. Equipment for air defense ranges from single reconnaissance planes to surveillance satellites and complex airborne warning and control systems (AWACS). AWACS planes, first flown by the Soviet Union and the United States in 1968, are high-speed jets outfitted with radar sensors, computers, and antennae to monitor a large combat area. Larger nations also use semi-automated ground environment systems, composed of computer and radar equipment, to scan for enemy radar signals and possible missile attacks.

Logistical commands direct the movement of troops and supplies. They primarily use large transport planes and helicopters for their duties. They also procure and maintain equipment. Training commands recruit men and women and use special training aircraft and weapons systems to prepare air force members for actual combat conditions.

TRAINING

Air force personnel can train for a variety of military careers, including those of pilot, technician, specialist, and instructor. New recruits go through basic training before specializing in a field of work. Future officers can attend special college and university programs, such as the Air Force Reserve Officer Training Corps (AFROTC) courses in the United States, or they can enroll in national service academies. In France, the air officer trainee studies at the École de l'Air (School of the Air) at Salon-de-Provence. In Great Britain, air force officer candidates train at the Royal Air Force College at Cranwell. United States Air Force cadets enroll at the United States Air Force Academy in Colorado Springs, Colo.

Training prepares air force members for actual warfare conditions. Pilots learn their trade in special trainer airplanes that simulate realistic combat flight conditions. This method of military pilot training was first devised by Maj. Robert Smith-Barry of the

UNITED STATES AIR FORCE ACADEMY

The United States Air Force Academy is a federally supported four-year institution of higher education that was founded in 1954. It primarily trains students for careers as Air Force officers. The academy is located on 18,000 acres (7,300 hectares) just outside of Colorado Springs, Colo. Males make up about three-quarters of the approximately 4,000 students, who are known as cadets. Women have been admitted as cadets since 1976.

Admission is highly competitive. Applicants must receive an official nomination, usually by a member

United States Air Force Academy chapel, outside of Colorado Springs, Colo. © Rich Grant/Denver Metro Convention & Visitors Bureau

of the U.S. Congress from their home state. Besides demonstrating academic excellence and leadership potential, cadets must be between the ages of 17 and 23, United States citizens, unmarried, without dependents, and in good physical condition. Incoming freshmen undergo a mentally and physically challenging summer training session before classes begin.

During the first two years, all students take part in a core curriculum, which includes military, physical, and leadership training in addition to academic studies. Students complete an academic major during the last two years. Areas of study include science, engineering, social sciences, and humanities. Air Force officers make up most of the faculty. Graduates receive a bachelor of science degree and a reserve commission as a second lieutenant in the Air Force. Cadets also receive flight training, which qualifies graduates in aerial navigation, entitling them to the position of an aircraft observer. If physically qualified, most graduates of the academy go to Air Force pilot training schools.

All students of the United States Air Force Academy are on full scholarship and receive a monthly stipend to cover supplies and personal expenses. Cadets wear uniforms and must live on campus for all years of study. All cadets must participate in athletics every semester, either through intramural sports or National Collegiate Athletic Association (NCAA) intercollegiate competition. The intercollegiate teams compete in the NCAA's Division I. The football team plays in the Football Bowl Subdivision. The school's nickname is the Falcons, and its colors are blue and silver.

British Royal Flying Corps. During World War I, when most air force trainees learned how to pilot by flying obsolete planes, Smith-Barry adapted the Avro 504J fighter craft with dual controls for both student and instructor. This paved the way for more efficient flying experience before combat.

During World War I, pilots went into action with about 20 hours of flying time in training. By the 21st century, they needed more than 400 hours and two years of training, reflecting the increased complexity of aircraft operation and maintenance.

CHAPTER 2

AIR POWER THROUGH WORLD WAR I

A ir power has been used for military purposes since the late 18th century. Although the Chinese may have used huge kites some 2,000 years ago to lift men into the skies for military reconnaissance, the first practical aircraft came much later.

EARLY AIRCRAFT

Brothers Joseph-Michel and Jacques-Étienne Montgolfier of France invented the first practical aircraft, the hot-air balloon, in 1783. This balloon was capable of rising to 6,000 feet (1,800 meters) and carried baskets to hold crews. This and other balloons were controlled by reheating air, releasing hydrogen gas, or eliminating ballast (weight). In 1793, the French government formed what may have been the world's first air force when it set up a corps of Aérostiers (Aeronauts) for the purpose of military observation from tethered balloons.

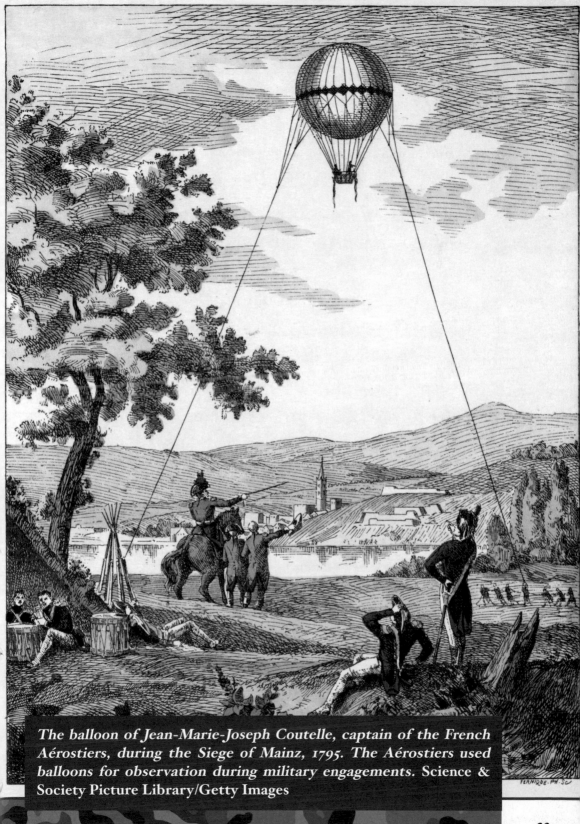

The balloon of Jean-Marie-Joseph Coutelle, captain of the French Aérostiers, during the Siege of Mainz, 1795. The Aérostiers used balloons for observation during military engagements. Science & Society Picture Library/Getty Images

BALLOONS

Balloons were first used as offensive weapons in 1849, when the Austrians unsuccessfully attempted to bombard Venice with bombs connected to time fuses. Hot-air balloons proved most useful as reconnaissance craft. This was demonstrated by their employment by both sides in the American Civil War (1861–65), by the British in Africa during the Boer War (1899–1902), and by the Russians in Japan during the Russo-Japanese War (1904–05).

Count Ferdinand von Zeppelin's airship, the LZ-1, in what was the first successful flight of a rigid airship, 1900. Science & Society Picture Library/Getty Images

In 1852, air power took a new direction with the first successful demonstration of the dirigible (steerable) balloon airship. Designed by the Frenchman Henri Giffard, the first dirigible was a nonrigid cylindrical-shaped airship composed of a gasbag, 144 feet (44 meters) long, propelled by a steam engine. This dirigible was the prototype of increasingly sophisticated craft, which promised more navigational control than that offered by wind-borne balloons.

AIRSHIPS AND AIRPLANES

True military aviation began with the perfection of the navigable airship and the airplane. In 1897, the Austrian David Schwartz designed the world's first rigid airship. It had an aluminum framework and was covered with aluminum sheeting. Although this craft was wrecked on a test flight, the rigid airship was subsequently improved by Count Ferdinand von Zeppelin of Germany. In 1900, Zeppelin built a huge cigar-shaped, metal-framed ship covered by a smooth cotton cloth, which he named the LZ-1. This ship, 420 feet (128 meters) long and driven by two 16-horsepower engines, was the

COUNT FERDINAND VON ZEPPELIN

Ferdinand von Zeppelin (1838–1917) was the first notable builder of rigid dirigible airships, for which his surname is still a popular generic term.

Zeppelin received a military commission in 1858. He made the first of several balloon ascensions at St. Paul, Minnesota, while acting as a military observer (1863) for the Union Army during the American Civil War. He saw military action in 1866 during the Seven Weeks' War and in 1870–71 during the Franco-German War, serving successively in the armies of Wüttemberg, Prussia, and imperial Germany. He retired in 1890 and devoted the rest of his life to the creation of the rigid airship for which he is known.

Zeppelin struggled for 10 years to produce his lighter-than-air craft. The initial flight (July 2, 1900) of the LZ-1 from a floating hangar on Lake Constance, near Friedrichshafen, Germany, was not entirely successful, but it had the effect of promoting the airship to the degree that public subscriptions and donations thereafter funded the count's work. The German government was quick to perceive the advantage of airships over the as yet poorly developed airplanes, and when Zeppelin achieved 24-hour flight in 1906, he received commissions for an entire fleet. More than 100 zeppelins were used for military operations in World War I. A passenger service known as Delag (Deutsche-Luftschiffahrts AG) was established in 1910, but Zeppelin died before attaining his goal of transcontinental flight.

forerunner of the more powerful Zeppelin craft used with some success by the Germans in World War I.

In 1903, the American brothers Wilbur and Orville Wright took the first controlled and sustained flight in a heavier-than-air craft, an airplane capable of flying at 30 miles (48 kilometers) per hour. Airplane experimentation soon flourished in other countries. Early models were distinguished by the number of wing levels. Monoplanes were designed with a single set of wings, biplanes had two sets of wings, and triplanes had three. Among the other early airplane pioneers was Louis Blériot of France. In 1907, he designed an airplane and flew more than 1/4 mile (400 meters), and in 1909, he demonstrated his type XI airplane with the first flight across the English Channel, a distance of about 25 miles (40 kilometers).

The Wright brothers had foreseen that the airplane would be a most useful machine for military reconnaissance. This prediction was first fulfilled on Oct. 23, 1911, during the Italo-Turkish War, when an Italian pilot made a one-hour reconnaissance flight over North Africa in a Blériot XI monoplane. Nine days later the Italians demonstrated another,

Louis Blériot pictured with his monoplane after he made the first successful flight across the English Channel in 1909. Bob Thomas/Popperfoto/Getty Images

deadlier use of the airplane, when they tossed heavy hand-grenade bombs from a plane flying over Libya. In 1912, the use of aircraft for psychological warfare was first demonstrated, when propaganda leaflets were showered over Libya from Italian planes.

Bombing techniques subsequently improved. Dummy bombs were dropped on a sea target in 1910 by Glenn Curtiss of the United States, and soon thereafter bomb carriers and bombsights were developed. The first bomb carrier consisted of a small rack, placed behind the observer's cockpit, in which small bombs were retained by a pin. The pin was removed over the target by pulling a string.

Soon airplanes were armed with other weapons. By 1910, work had begun on the installation of machine guns. In 1913, Col. Isaac Newton Lewis of the United States went to Belgium to manufacture his Lewis gun, which was a low-recoil weapon that was to come into widespread use in fighter planes that flew during World War I.

By 1911, deteriorating international relations led many countries to build up military capacity, including air fleets. In this period the first air forces were organized. They were established as subordinate divisions within existing armies.

WORLD WAR I

At the outbreak of World War I, Germany led the world in air power with 260 airplanes and a fleet of 14 Zeppelins. Other allies of Germany, including Italy, also had newly formed air arms. The British had about 100 aircraft at this time; the French, backed by the world's leading aviation industry, had 156. Some 100,000 aircraft flew in the war, primarily in support of ground and sea troops.

During the war, rapid advances were made in both air power strategy and technology. In 1914, the airplanes mobilized for war were flimsy, kitelike structures powered by engines of uncertain power. At best, they could climb 2,000 to 3,000 feet (600 to 900 meters) and fly at speeds of 60 to 70 miles (95 to 110 kilometers) per hour. At worst, they could barely get off the ground. Only four years later, single-seat airplane fighters with 150- to 200-horsepower engines were outfitted with machine guns to do battle at 15,000 feet (4,600 meters) in the air.

The aircraft that were developed during World War I were of three main types, each with its own specific purpose. These airplanes were reconnaissance craft, fighter planes, and bombers.

RECONNAISSANCE CRAFT

The use of aircraft for reconnaissance was probably the most important contribution of air power to the war effort. In the first weeks of hostilities, French aircraft spotted the movements of the German First Army, and this led to the Battle of the Marne. The Germans, in turn, successfully used Zeppelin airships to monitor their opponents'—the Allies'—shipping movements. By 1917, these craft could stay in the air for more than 95 hours at a time.

The British revived interest in nonrigid airships with their design of the blimp (from "British" Class B Airship and "limp," that is, nonrigid). Hundreds of blimps were built during the war for antisubmarine convoy and coastal patrol work.

Reconnaissance techniques were greatly improved during World War I. Photography was added to visual observation by the British in 1914, when pictures were taken of German troop positions during the first battle of the Aisne. Radio came into use at this time as a means of passing messages between reconnaissance aircraft and ground personnel.

At the start of the war, reconnaissance craft were usually unarmed, except for the rifles and pistols carried by fliers. Soon the realization that these craft were vulnerable to attack led to the widespread adoption of the

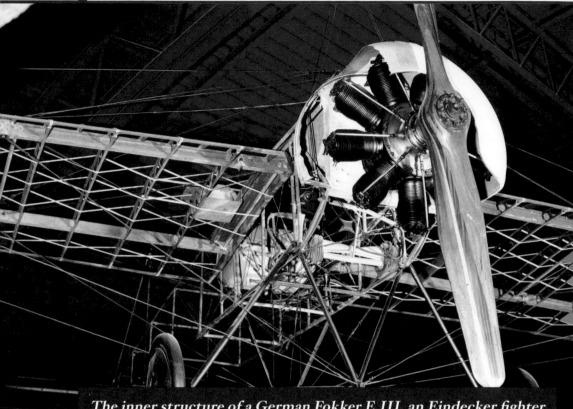

The inner structure of a German Fokker E.III, an Eindecker fighter plane used by Germany during World War I. Science & Society Picture Library/Getty Images

fighter plane—an aircraft designed to attack enemy reconnaissance and bombing aircraft.

FIGHTER PLANES

Fighter planes were pioneered by Britain, which in 1913 had developed the Vickers *Destroyer*, a fighting biplane. In 1915, the French adapted the interrupter to a Morane-Saulnier monoplane. This gun synchronizer allowed machine gun bullets to pass between the blades of a spinning propeller.

When a French fighter plane was shot down by the Germans in 1915, the Dutch designer Anthony Fokker used the captured French craft as a model for his Fokker Eindecker, a single-seat fighter that was to give the German Luftwaffe (air force) temporary air superiority on the Western Front. From October 1915 until May 1916, Fokker Eindeckers blasted the French and British from the skies, a mastery that was ended only when the Allied forces improved their own fighter craft in 1916. In that year the British developed D.H.2 and F.E.2b "pusher" fighters. These airplanes were fitted with one or more nose-fixed guns that fired forward, and the pilot could aim his aircraft as a firing weapon.

The aerial warfare made possible by these fighting airplanes led to individual combat in dogfights, one-on-one battles between pilots who used machine guns against enemy fliers. The war produced hundreds of flying aces, pilots who were credited with shooting down five or more enemy aircraft. Among the most famous were Capt. Edward ("Eddie") Rickenbacker of the United States, Baron Manfred von Richthofen of Germany, René

Fonck of France, and Edward Mannock of Great Britain. These pilots also introduced the strategy of flying planes in a "circus" formation, or an air armada. The flying circus led to enormous air battles involving more than 100 fighter planes at a time.

A related development was the building of aircraft carriers to launch fighter planes from platforms built over battleship gun turrets. Some aircraft carriers were merely barges that were towed behind high-speed destroyers.

BOMBERS

A third type of aircraft developed during the war was the bomber. After 1915, both sides used bombers to attack enemy targets, such as railway stations and weapons storehouses. These targets were deep behind enemy lines and out of the range of conventional ground troops.

The Germans used their Zeppelin aircraft as strategic bombers during the war, launching raids against London and other European cities. But Zeppelins proved to be too vulnerable, and by 1916, the Germans were building bomber airplanes.

The German Gotha biplanes of 1916 had a wingspan of nearly 90 feet (27 meters) and two engines of 260 horsepower each. The Gothas could carry a 2,000-pound (900-kilogram) bombload and fly 300 miles (480 kilometers) without refueling. Even larger was the Siemens-Schückert R-VIII, a bomber with a wingspread of more than 150 feet (45 meters) and powered by six 300-horsepower engines.

The Russians, British, and French also developed bomber airplanes. In 1915, Igor Sikorsky of Russia designed the first successful four-engined airplane. The British contributed the twin-engined Handley Page, the first heavy bomber used by British and American forces. The Voisin bomber of France was also in service in World War I. Known as the "chicken coop" because of its profusion of struts and wires, the Voisin type L had an 80-horsepower engine and could carry 130 pounds (58 kilograms) of bombs to be hand dropped overboard by the flier.

While large numbers of aircraft were used in World War I, they exercised little direct influence on the outcome of the conflict. The importance of air power in this war was rather in the development of increasingly sophisticated types of aircraft and of new strategic policies, which would be significant for military use in the later wars of the 20th century.

CHAPTER 3

AIR POWER FROM C. 1918 TO 1945

During the years between World Wars I and II, national air forces emerged around the world. There were also a number of tremendous advances in aircraft technology and strategy.

THE INTERWAR YEARS

Immediately after World War I progress was slow. This was because there was a surplus of airplanes during peacetime, and governments were reluctant to spend money on the development of new military aircraft. Moreover, the Treaty of Versailles forbade the Germans to arm for military purposes, and what had been one of the world's most powerful air forces was disbanded.

NEW STRATEGIC CONCEPTS

Two important strategic concepts were shaped in this period. The first was the doctrine of strategic bombing. The Italian brigadier general Giulio Douhet argued in *The Command of the Air*, an influential work that was first published in 1921, that future wars would be won by huge formations of bomber planes striking deep into enemy territory against industrial targets and civilian population centers. This would, Douhet stated, disrupt production and destroy national morale. The need for this kind of air power meant that nations should concentrate their military resources to build up powerful independent air forces with which to defeat their enemies without the aid of land or sea power.

This idea of the independent air force was the second important air power concept of the interwar era. Supporters included the British general Hugh Montague Trenchard and the American general William (Billy) Mitchell. Mitchell claimed that the airplane was the most important instrument of war, and that the failure of United States military leaders to expand the air force amounted to no less than "criminal negligence." Mitchell's outspoken views led to his court-martial in 1925. But his vision of the future of air power proved to be correct.

In Britain the Royal Air Force was firmly established as an independent power by 1923,

WILLIAM MITCHELL

One of the most accurate military prophets of the 20th century, Gen. William (Billy) Mitchell (1879–1936), predicted as early as 1921 that air supremacy would win the next war. In 1925, he was court-martialed for insubordination. But World War II confirmed Mitchell's theories on air power. In 1942, six years after his death, Congress voted to restore his name to the Army rolls with the rank of major general.

William Mitchell was born on Dec. 29, 1879, in Nice, France. When he was 3 years old his parents returned to their family home near Milwaukee, Wis. His father, John Mitchell, later became a United States senator.

When the United States declared war on Spain, Mitchell enlisted in the Army as a private. He quickly advanced to the rank of second lieutenant in the Signal Corps.

Mitchell became interested in flying when he witnessed Orville and Wilbur Wright's first demonstration of a military plane at Fort Myer, Va., in 1908. Six years later Orville Wright taught Mitchell to fly. In 1917, during World War I, Mitchell organized and later was given command of the United States Air Force in France. At that time the Air Force was a branch of the Signal Corps. Mitchell was made a brigadier general.

Following the armistice, Mitchell became assistant chief of the Air Service. In 1921, he proved that bombers could sink even the largest naval vessels of the time. He constantly criticized the military high command for not developing American air power. As a result he was reduced to the rank of colonel. When a Navy dirigible was lost in 1925, Mitchell charged high officers with "criminal negligence." His court-martial for insubordination followed. Rather than accept a five-year suspension from the Army, Mitchell resigned. As a private citizen he continued his appeal for adequate air power. He died in New York City on Feb. 19, 1936.

He did not live to see the fulfillment during World War II of many of his prophecies: strategic bombing, mass airborne operations, and

Gen. William (Billy) Mitchell. Interim Archives/ Archive Photos/Getty Images

the eclipse of the battleship by the bomb-carrying military airplane. In 1946, the U.S. Congress authorized a special medal in his honor; it was presented to his son in 1948 by Gen. Carl Spaatz, chief of staff of the newly created U.S. Air Force.

when the government began an air defense program. The Italians established their Regia Aeronautica in 1923. The French followed in 1928 with an air ministry and later with the creation of the Armée de l'Air. In 1935, restrictions against German rearmament ended, and Adolf Hitler established the Luftwaffe as an independent military service. In the United States, the Soviet Union, and Japan, air arms remained under the control of previously established military branches.

TECHNOLOGICAL DEVELOPMENTS

Perhaps the most important technical improvement in this era was the development of jet propulsion. In 1930, Frank Whittle of Great Britain patented the first jet engine. On Aug. 27, 1939, the first flight of a jet-powered aircraft was made by a Heinkel He-178 airplane in Germany.

Rocket research also began in the inter-war years. Both the Germans and the Soviets were experimenting with rocket-powered aircraft by 1930, and, in the United States, Robert Goddard was researching liquid-fueled rockets in New Mexico.

The military airplane was completely transformed between the world wars. Wood construction gave way to metal. Typical of the new fighter craft was the British Supermarine Spitfire, first flown in 1936. Its metal structure and a new type of machine armament on the wings to eliminate the need for bulky interrupter gear made it an advanced craft for its time.

In 1931, the Boeing Airplane Company of the United States built the B-9 bomber. Also of all-metal design, it was a great improvement over all previous bombers. In 1932, the Martin B-10 added enclosed cockpits and an internal weapons bay for further structural improvement.

In 1935, the Boeing B-17 was flight-tested. This was the prototype for the Flying Fortress, the bombardment mainstay of World War II. By the late 1930s, bombers and fighter planes were equipped with bulletproof windshields, armor plating, gun turrets, and radar attachments.

As airplane technology advanced in these ways, the airship received a blow from which it never recovered. In May 1937, the German passenger dirigible *Hindenburg* exploded at the Lakehurst (N.J.) Naval Air Station, killing 35 people. With its destruction, the era of the great dirigible balloons passed.

During the 1930s, air power was increasingly a factor in wars throughout the world. The British used air power in colonial conflicts in Iraq, Aden, and India; and the Italians used a tactical air force against Ethiopia in 1935. In the Spanish Civil War (1936–39), the air forces of Italy and Germany supported Gen. Francisco Franco with the bombing of cities, including Barcelona, Madrid, and Guernica. Japan mounted an air attack against China in a 1931 dispute over the control of Manchuria. By the time the Germans used air power in their invasions of Czechoslovakia and Poland in 1938 and 1939, it was evident that air power had come into its own.

WORLD WAR II

Air power was a decisive factor in the outcome of World War II. An early German lead in air power was overcome by Allied advances in both radar technology and the use of strategic weapons.

At the start of the war in September 1939, the German Luftwaffe was the best equipped air force in the world, with some 500,000 air force personnel and about 5,000 aircraft. In contrast, the British Royal Air Force (RAF) was composed of some 100,000 men and some 2,000 aircraft.

STRATEGIC BOMBING

Strategic bombing became an early part of the war effort. The Germans successfully used intensive bombing raids to assault Norway, The Netherlands, Belgium, and France. Luftwaffe bombers destroyed Allied cities and transportation networks and flew in support of advancing German ground troops.

In the Battle of Britain in the summer of 1940, British RAF forces of about 600 aircraft, mostly Hawker Hurricanes and Supermarine Spitfires, faced over 2,700 Luftwaffe planes, including the powerful Junkers JU-87 Stuka dive-bomber. But this imbalance was overcome by pioneering developments in British radar, which allowed the RAF to manage its aircraft efficiently by using an early-warning system. As a result, the RAF was largely responsible for preventing a German invasion of England.

THE BATTLE OF BRITAIN

The Battle of Britain during World War II involved the successful defense of Great Britain against unremitting and destructive air raids conducted by the German air force (Luftwaffe) from July through September 1940, after the fall of France. Victory for the Luftwaffe in the air battle would have exposed Great Britain to invasion by the German army, which was then in control of the ports of France only a few miles away across the English Channel. In the event, the battle was won by the Royal Air Force (RAF) Fighter Command, whose victory not only blocked the possibility of invasion but also created the conditions for Great Britain's survival, for the extension of the war, and for the eventual defeat of Nazi Germany.

Beginning with bomber attacks against shipping on July 10 and continuing into early August, a rising stream of air attacks by the Luftwaffe was delivered against British convoys and ports. Then, on August 13, the main offensive—called Adlerangriff ("Eagle Attack") by German leader Adolf Hitler—was unleashed, initially against air bases but also against aircraft factories and against radar stations in southeastern England. Although targets and tactics were changed in different phases, the underlying object was always to wear down Britain's air defense, and indeed the effort severely strained the limited resources of Fighter Command. The British disposed slightly more than 600 frontline fighters to defend the country. The Germans meanwhile made available about 1,300 bombers and dive-bombers and about 900 single-engine and 300 twin-engine fighters.

Smoke rising from the London Docklands after the first mass air raid on the British capital, Sept. 7, 1940. New Times Paris Bureau Collection/USIA/NARA

The British, however, found themselves fighting with the unexpected advantage of superior equipment. The British radar early-warning system, called Chain Home, was the most advanced and the most operationally adapted system in the world. Even while suffering from frequent attacks by the Luftwaffe, it largely prevented German bomber formations from exploiting the element of surprise. To fight off the bombers, Fighter Command employed squadrons of durable and heavily armed Hawker Hurricanes, preferring to save the faster and more agile Supermarine Spitfire—unsurpassed as an interceptor by any fighter in any other air force—for use against the bombers' fighter escorts. German bombers lacked the bomb load capacity to strike permanently devastating blows, and they also proved, in daylight, to be easily vulnerable to the British fighters. By late August, the Luftwaffe had lost more than 600 aircraft and the RAF only 260.

In addition to technology, Britain had the advantage of fighting against an enemy that had no systematic or consistent plan of action. At the beginning of September, the Germans dropped some bombs, apparently by accident, on civilian areas in London, and the British retaliated by unexpectedly launching a bombing raid on Berlin.

By mid-September, Fighter Command had demonstrated that the Luftwaffe could not gain air ascendancy over Britain. British fighters were shooting down German bombers faster than German industry could produce them. To avoid the deadly RAF fighters, the Luftwaffe shifted almost entirely to night raids on Britain's industrial centres. The "Blitz," as the night raids came to be called, would cause many deaths and great hardship for the civilian population, but it contributed little to the main purpose of the air offensive—to dominate the skies in advance of an invasion of England. The date of invasion had been deferred to September 21. On October 12 Hitler announced that the operation was off for the winter, and long before the arrival of spring he decided to turn eastward against Russia. Plans for an invasion were definitively discarded; the campaign against Britain henceforth became purely a blockade of its sea approaches, conducted mainly by submarines and only supplemented by the Luftwaffe.

The German air raids on London in 1940 and 1941 further demonstrated the potential of strategic bombing. For over a month in the fall of 1940, German bombers dropped nearly 14,000 tons (12,700 metric tons) of high explosives and more than 12,000 incendiary canisters on the city. These attacks subsided as Germany became engaged on other fronts, particularly with the Soviet Union.

At the same time, Allied forces were developing improved aircraft able to match

Flying Fortresses, the B-17s of the United States 8th Air Force's 3rd Air Division, bomb German communications and transportation systems at Chemnitz on Feb. 6, 1945. © AP Images

those of the Luftwaffe. The Americans pro-
duced the Boeing B-17 Flying Fortress day
bomber and the four-engine B-24 Liberator.
By 1942, the British had added the Bristol
Beaufighter long-range fighter and the Avro
Lancaster, a four-engined heavy bomber.

By 1943, the Allied bombing offensive led
to the around-the-clock bombing of Germany,
shifting the balance of air power away from
the Luftwaffe. The United States bombed
German cities by day, and the RAF continued the assault at night. By 1945 this bombing
strategy had caused some 600,000 casualties and inflicted great damage on German
cities, including Dresden, Hamburg, Essen,
and Berlin. On March 11, 1945, 1,079 United
States Eighth Air Force planes released 4,738
tons (4,298 metric tons) of explosives on
Essen. This was the greatest weight of bombs
dropped on a single target in Europe.

On the Pacific Front the Japanese displayed
an awesome use of airmanship with the surprise
attack on the American fleet at Pearl Harbor,
Hawaii, on Dec. 7, 1941. They crippled 8 battle-
ships, 10 warships, and 349 aircraft, and killed
or wounded 3,581 troops. By 1944, the Allies
had countered with systematic bombing raids
over Japan. These raids utilized the Boeing B-29

CURTIS LEMAY

Entering the U.S. Army Air Corps in 1928, Curtis LeMay (1906–90) advanced to the position of bombardment group commander by 1942. Flying with the 8th Air Force from England (1942–44), he became known for his development of advanced bomber tactics, including pattern bombing and the combat box formation. After commanding B-29s in India and China (1944), LeMay took over the 21st Bomber Command in the Mariana Islands (January 1945); in that post he planned and originated the low-altitude incendiary-bombing tactics that burned out parts of Tokyo and a number of other Japanese cities in an effort to force a surrender before the Allied invasion of Japan, which was planned for the end of that year.

After the war LeMay commanded the U.S. air forces in Europe, and in that capacity he directed the Berlin airlift in 1948. He headed the U.S. Strategic Air Command from 1948 to 1957 and built it into a global strike force. He was promoted to the rank of general in 1951. In 1957, he was named vice chief of staff and four years later chief of staff of the U.S. Air Force. He retired in 1965.

In 1968, he was the vice presidential candidate on the third-party (American Independent) ticket headed by George C. Wallace.

Superfortress, a long-range bomber operating from bases in China and later from islands in the central Pacific.

In 1945, United States Maj. Gen. Curtis E. LeMay of the 20th Bomber Command ordered his Superforts to attack Japanese industrial centers with firebombs. Seventeen strikes totaling 6,960 flights dropped 41,600 tons (37,700 metric tons) of incendiaries and set afire 102 square miles (264 square kilometers) of Tokyo, Nagoya, Kobe, Osaka, and Yokohama.

In 1944 and 1945, the Japanese tried a new tactic. Kamikaze (Divine Wind) pilots, believing in the Shinto philosophy of honorable death in battle, committed suicide by diving bomb-laden Mitsubishi A6M planes into sea targets. These kamikaze attacks sank 34 ships and damaged 288 others.

Air power was decisive in battles on other fronts, including the Mediterranean, where British air forces supported Gen. Bernard Montgomery's march to Tripoli. Allied air forces also contributed to the German collapse in North Africa in 1943.

In the Soviet Union, inferior equipment and training allowed German air supremacy

KAMIKAZE

The term *kamikaze* refers to any of the Japanese pilots who in World War II made deliberate suicidal crashes into enemy targets, usually ships. It also denotes the aircraft used in such attacks. The practice was most prevalent from the Battle of Leyte Gulf, October 1944, to the end of the war. The word *kamikaze* means "divine wind," a reference to a typhoon that fortuitously dispersed a Mongol invasion fleet threatening Japan from the west in 1281. Most kamikaze planes were ordinary fighters or light bombers, usually loaded with bombs and extra gasoline tanks before being flown deliberately to crash into their targets.

A kamikaze pilot tying the signature kamikaze headband—worn during the final mission—around his head. The image on the headband represents the rising sun. Keystone/Hulton Archive/Getty Images

A piloted missile was developed for kamikaze use that was given the nickname "Baka" by the Allies from the Japanese word for fool. The pilot had no means of getting out once the missile was fastened to the aircraft that would launch it. Dropped usually from an altitude of over 25,000 feet (7,500 meters) and more than 50 miles (80 kilometers) from its target, the missile would glide to about 3 miles (5 kilometers) from its target before the pilot turned on its three rocket engines, accelerating the craft to more than 600 miles (960 kilometers) per hour in its final dive. The explosive charge built into the nose weighed more than a ton.

Kamikaze attacks sank 34 ships and damaged hundreds of others during the war. At Okinawa they inflicted the greatest losses ever suffered by the U.S. Navy in a single battle, killing almost 5,000 men. Usually the most successful defense against kamikaze attack was to station picket destroyers around capital ships and direct the destroyers' antiaircraft batteries against the kamikazes as they approached the larger vessels.

on the Eastern Front until 1944. By then the Soviet air force was able to dominate in clashes with the Luftwaffe. In the spring of 1945, the Soviet air force devastated Berlin with more than 7,500 bombers.

ADVANCES IN AIRCRAFT

While bombers were used extensively in World War II, other aircraft also had a great impact. Planes used for tactical support contributed to the Allied landing at Normandy on June 6, 1944, when United States forces flew more than 8,000 sorties in support of the operation. By that time Allied forces had won air superiority over most of Europe.

Fighter planes, used to battle enemy fighters and attack enemy bombers, increased in speed during the war. Among the first small high-speed strike aircraft was the heavily armored Soviet Ilyushin IL-2 Shturmovik. In 1943 and 1944, American P-47 and P-51 fighters, equipped with external fuel tanks, flew long-range cover for heavy bombers. These fighters were in great part responsible for gaining Allied air superiority over Europe. Jet and rocket-powered planes in use by 1944 boosted fighter speeds from about 350 miles (565 kilometers) per hour to 600 miles (965 kilometers) per hour. The first jet fighter, the Gloster Meteor, was put into operation by the RAF in 1944. The Germans soon followed with the Messerschmitt ME-262 twin jet fighter.

In 1944, the Germans used V-1 flying bombs and, later, V-2 rockets carrying high explosives to threaten British cities. These bombs caused considerable damage for a short period but were developed too late to play a major role in the war. Allied forces bombed the launching sites in northern Europe and overran them soon after the Allied invasion of Europe in June 1944. These early rockets were prototypes for the guided missiles of the postwar era.

Reconnaissance developments included the use of streamlined high-speed fighter planes that sped low over enemy targets to take photographs and then escaped homeward at maximum speed. High-altitude craft took photographs on motion-picture film that was later processed into mosaic large-scale maps, foreshadowing developments in aerial mapmaking.

Air transport advances during the war included the use of airborne parachute troops dropped by plane into combat areas. The German air force first tried this technique during the Battle of Crete in May 1941, using the Junkers JU-52 transport plane and troop-carrying gliders.

World War II ended in 1945. The war in Europe came to an end in May, when the German forces surrendered to the Allies. The war in the Pacific ended in August with the bombing of two Japanese cities. On August 6 a B-29, the *Enola Gay*, dropped an

Col. Paul W. Tibbets, Jr., pilot of the Enola Gay, *the plane that dropped the atomic bomb on Hiroshima, Japan, Aug. 6, 1945.* National Archives/Hulton Archive/Getty Images

atomic bomb on Hiroshima, and three days later another B-29 dropped an atomic bomb on Nagasaki. The next day the Japanese surrendered to the United States forces.

CHAPTER 4

AIR POWER FROM C. 1950 TO C. 1991

Toward the end of World War II, the first operational jet fighter, the German Me-262, outflew the best Allied escorts while attacking bomber formations. This introduced the jet age, in which aircraft soon flew at more than twice the speed of sound (741 miles [1,193 kilometers] per hour at sea level and 659 miles [1,061 kilometers] per hour at 36,000 feet [10,973 meters]) and easily climbed to altitudes of 50,000 feet (15, 240 meters). At the same time, advanced electronics removed the task of early warning from the pilot's eye, and guided missiles extended the range of aerial combat, at least in theory, to beyond visual range.

THE KOREAN WAR

The conflict over the control of Korea, fought from 1950 to 1953, was between the Democratic People's Republic of Korea

(North Korea), supported by the Soviet Union and China, and the Republic of Korea (South Korea), supported by United Nations (UN) forces dominated by the United States. Both sides suppressed the use of all-out air power strategies in an effort to avoid a world war.

Air power during the Korean War was used only against precise targets in a limited area of conflict. Bombers attacked bridges, roads, and industrial centers, while planes such as the B-26 flew in support of ground armies. The UN forces limited the air power capacity of the North Koreans by destroying their air bases as they neared completion.

The first jet fighter battles were fought in this war, as Republic F-84 Thunderjets, Lockheed P-80C Shooting Stars, and North American F-86 Sabres faced Mikoyan MiG-15's in the skies over Korea. The first heavy jet bomber, the Boeing B-47 Stratofortress, was in use by 1951. Another important development in Korea was the use of the helicopter in warfare. Helicopters were used to transport men, supplies, and guns to otherwise inaccessible places. They were also used to fire rockets and other missiles. They could evacuate casualties quickly, resulting in a

F-86

Also called Sabre or Sabrejet, the F-86 is a single-seat, single-engine jet fighter built for the U.S. by North American Aviation, Inc., the first jet fighter in the West to exploit aerodynamic principles learned from German engineering at the close of World War II. The F-86 was built with the wings swept back in order to reduce transonic drag rise as flight speed approached the sound barrier, and it was capable of exceeding the speed of sound in a dive. A prototype was first flown in October 1947, and the first squadron became operational in 1949. In December 1950, U.S. pilots flying F-86s began history's first large-scale jet fighter combat against Soviet-built MiG-15s in Korea. Though inferior to the MiG-15 in weight of arma- ment, turn radius, and maximum speed at combat

A flight line with F-86 Sabres being prepared for combat in the Korean War. Interim Archives/Archive Photos/Getty Images

altitude, the F-86 quickly established supremacy over its Soviet adversary, in part because of its superior handling characteristics. In September 1958, Sabres flown by Chinese Nationalists (also against MiG-15s) became the first jets to fire guided air-to-air missiles in combat. The last one built was delivered to the United States Air Force in December 1956.

The F-86 had a wingspan of 37 feet 1 inch (11.3 meters) and a length of 37 feet 6 inches (11.45 meters). Powered by a series of General Electric turbojet engines generating 5,000 to 9,000 pounds (22 to 40 kilonewtons) of thrust, it had a top speed of almost 700 miles (1,100 kilometers) per hour in level flight and a maximum service altitude approaching 50,000 feet (15,000 meters). Besides missiles, its armament included .50-inch machine guns or 20-millimetre cannon in the fuselage and rockets or bombs under the wings.

reduction of the death rate to the lowest figure in modern military history.

THE VIETNAM WAR

United States military involvement in Indochina began in 1961, when American troops entered Vietnam as advisers in a conflict between the South Vietnamese government and Communist rebels. By 1965, United States military forces were heavily engaged in attacks on the Viet Cong and North Vietnamese targets.

The use of air power in this war, as in Korea, was primarily for tactical support. Air Force pilots used fighter and bomber planes to destroy enemy supplies, support ground troops, and deliver both supplies and personnel. American pilots also dropped defoliants—chemical substances that destroy plant life—over the countryside. They hoped in this way to deny the cover of trees to guerrilla fighters. Unmanned drone planes were used to penetrate bombed areas at high speeds and photograph earlier strikes.

The high cost and complex operation requirements of jet planes made the use of less powerful aircraft more expedient. In Vietnam the A-4 Skyhawk, with a maximum speed of 685 miles (1,102 kilometers) per hour, proved most effective for tactical support.

The Boeing B-52 jet bomber was also used during this conflict. First used in 1955, the B-52 was a huge jet airplane with a range greater than 12,000 miles (19,300 kilometers), a wingspan of 185 feet (56 meters), and speeds of up to 630 miles (1,015 kilometers) per hour. Among the high-technology

B-52

Also called Stratofortress, the B-52 is a U.S. long-range heavy bomber, designed by the Boeing Company in 1948, first flown in 1952, and first delivered for military service in 1955. Though originally intended to be an atomic-bomb carrier capable of reaching the Soviet Union, it has proved adaptable to a number of missions, and B-52s remained in service well into the 21st century. The B-52 has a wingspan of 185 feet (56 metres)

Boeing B-52 Stratofortress, a U.S. high-altitude bomber, dropping a stream of bombs over Vietnam. U.S. Air Force

and a length of 160 feet 10.9 inches (49 metres). It is powered by eight jet engines mounted under the wings in four twin pods. The plane's maximum speed at 55,000 feet (17,000 metres) is Mach 0.9 (595 miles [960 kilometers] per hour); at only a few hundred feet above the ground, it can fly at Mach 0.5 (375 miles [600 kilometers] per hour). It originally carried a crew of six, its sole defensive armament being a remotely controlled gun turret in the tail. In 1991, the gun was eliminated and the crew reduced to five.

weapons it carried were precision guided munitions (PGMs), including the "smart bomb"—an explosive directed to its target by the use of a laser beam.

Air power advances were made in the development of short-takeoff-and-landing (STOL) craft, which reduced the need for long concrete runways, and in counterinsurgency aircraft (COIN), designed to operate from rough terrain. Helicopters were used in an air patrol system that also employed transport planes. The air patrol system brought mobility to ground troops by transporting men, guns, ammunition, and supplies to remote locations. In October 1965, the relief of an outpost was accomplished by the arrival of a whole division in helicopters.

The main use of strategic bombing occurred in December 1971 and in April 1972. United States Air Force (USAF) Strategic Air Command pilots blanketed Hanoi and Haiphong in North Vietnam with bombs dropped from B-52s in an intensive series of raids. As in Korea, the lesson in Indochina was that conventional bombing and fighter strategies would not by themselves win a guerrilla war.

WARS IN THE MIDDLE EAST

Several conflicts in the Middle East between Israel and its Arab neighbors have been shaped by the use of air power. The Suez crisis of 1956 began when British, French, and Israeli forces dominated Egyptian airspace by using fighter and bomber aircraft as a tactical support force for advancing ground troops. Within two days the Egyptian air force was destroyed. In 1967, the Six-Day War between Egypt and Israel was won by the superior air strategy of Israel. Both Egypt and Israel had equal air forces, though Egypt could call upon the military resources of other Arab nations. But in three hours, on

Israeli paratroopers marching in 1973 during the Yom Kippur War.
Getty Images

June 5, 1967, the Israeli air force completed a preemptive strike against Egyptian airfields. This attack, along with raids on the airfields of Syria, Jordan, and Iraq, led to Israel's eventual victory.

At the start of the Yom Kippur War of October 1973, a surprise strike by Arab forces killed more than 2,500 Israelis and destroyed a fifth of their air fleet. While Israel countered with the use of paratroopers, ground tank forces, and conventional air power to end the war, the Egyptian use of missiles reduced the effectiveness of Israeli air efforts.

THE PERSIAN GULF WAR

The importance of destroying enemy air defenses and establishing supremacy in the air in order to assert mastery on the ground was reinforced during the Operation Desert Storm air offensive of the Persian Gulf War (1990–91). Allied air forces, led by the United States Air Force and Navy but including hundreds of French, British, Saudi, and Kuwaiti planes, had three objectives: to win air supremacy, to destroy strategic targets, and to degrade Iraqi ground forces in preparation for driving them out of occupied Kuwait.

On Jan. 17, 1991, the allies launched an intense bombing campaign, and by January 28 they had gained air supremacy. The Iraqi air defense system of aircraft, surface-to-air missiles, antiaircraft guns, and ground-controlled interception radars was rendered ineffective by air strikes and the use of stealth technology. Iraqi losses included some 35 aircraft downed in air-to-air combat, some 100 destroyed on the ground, and 115 flown to Iran to avoid destruction. Allied losses totaled only 39 aircraft, none in air combat. The allied air forces then destroyed targets vital to the Iraqi war effort. These included command, control, and communications facilities; ammunition; chemical and biological weapons facilities; petroleum, oil, and lubricant stockpiles; and manufacturing plants. Allied air forces also engaged in search-and-destroy missions against mobile launchers for Iraq's Scud missiles.

Continuing the air war in order to maximize Iraqi, and minimize allied, casualties, the allied air forces disabled some 30 percent of Iraqi ground forces in the combat zone before the launching of the Operation Desert Sabre ground assault. Operation Desert Sabre lasted only 100 hours. Large numbers of Iraqi troops surrendered without fighting, collapsing under the cumulative effects of the allies' prolonged massive air bombardment and the concentrated firepower and speed of the ground attack.

AIR POWER IN THE MISSILE AGE

One of the most important developments after World War II was the achievement of supersonic flight. On Oct. 14, 1947, Maj. Charles Yeager of the USAF became the first person to fly faster than the speed of sound. He made his historic flight in a Bell X-1 rocket-powered airplane. The Soviets also broke the sound barrier in 1947, using the MiG-15 fighter. By the time of the Korean War, fighters could fly at supersonic speeds of Mach 2, or twice the speed of sound. By 1959, planes such as the Mirage III and the Lockheed F-104 could fly as fast as 1,650 miles (2,655 kilometers) per hour. The SR-71 Blackbird reconnaissance aircraft routinely flew missions at Mach 3 and at altitudes of more than 80,000 feet (24,000 meters). Perhaps the greatest of the experimental supersonic planes was the North American X-15 rocket plane, which could reach a speed of Mach 6.72 (4,689 miles, or 7,546 kilometers, per hour). The National Aerospace Plane/X-30, developed by the U.S. Defense Advanced Research Projects Agency (DARPA), was intended to fly at Mach 25 (17,445 miles, or 28,074 kilometers, per hour), but the project was abandoned in 1995 due to cost overruns and the obsolescence of high-speed reconnaissance planes.

Although missiles have to some degree made the heavy bomber obsolete, the United States and a few other nations retain long-range supersonic bombers equipped with automatic navigation and electronic countermeasure (ECM) systems. These automated systems arose because supersonic speeds in aircraft made the human navigation and control of the planes extremely difficult. Aircraft control was made easier with the development of avionics, the use of electronic aids in aviation.

In addition, "fly-by-wire" systems—which interpreted the movement of the pilot's control stick and used computers to translate that action into stable flight—were of critical importance for some advanced aircraft. The F-117 Stealth Fighter was especially notable in this respect. Its unorthodox shape, designed to minimize its radar signature, made it inherently unstable in the air,

Maj. Charles Yeager, holding a model of the Bell X-1 airplane he famously flew when he first broke the sound barrier. Hulton Archive/ Getty Images

AVIONICS

Avionics (derived from the expression "aviation electronics") is the development and production of electronic instruments for use in aviation and astronautics. The term also refers to the instruments themselves. Avionics relies on the use of miniature electronic components and computer and radar technology to automate navigation and weapons systems. For example, avionic-equipped jets can be flown on preset courses, while radar searches for and "locks onto" enemy aircraft. After firing at the most favorable moment, the electronic fighter can break away to return to base. The devices used for this kind of detection, pursuit, and destruction of enemy aircraft are also used for ECM devices, which attempt to disable enemy countermeasures and jam radar.

but the plane's flight computers corrected for its aerodynamic idiosyncrasies and kept it flying until its retirement in 2008.

DEVELOPMENTS IN LONG-RANGE CAPABILITIES

The external design of aircraft has changed as flying speeds have increased. Swept-back wings and delta plane forms replaced the straight or tapered wings of World War

II. By the early 1990s, variable-geometry arrangements—to allow wing flexibility—had been developed.

Long-range capabilities of postwar aircraft were further extended with the growth of aerial refueling. In 1949, the Boeing B-50 *Lucky Lady II* flew nonstop around the world in 94 hours, proving the feasibility of aerial refueling for long-range missions. In another demonstration of in-flight refueling, two Republic F-84-E Thunderjet fighters flew across the Atlantic in 1950 in just over ten hours, completing the first nonstop, transoceanic jet flight.

Missile development began in earnest in the early 1950s, when both the Soviets and the Americans introduced their first missiles. For decades these two nations continued to seek equality in military strength by balancing and counterbalancing various types of offensive and defensive missile forces. In air defense, where missiles have an irreplaceable role, fighter-interceptor aircraft also play a part. Airborne for long periods, they can meet attacking aircraft or missiles far from the target. In strategic warfare, bombers and missiles complement one another.

The manned bomber is flexible. It can be recalled or directed to switch targets. Its crew

U.S. Air Force F-15 Eagle fighter over Iraq. TSGT Jack Braden, USAF

can take radar-map pictures of the area it has destroyed and use them to plan subsequent missions. Jet bombers can carry far heavier and more varied loads of explosives than can earlier types of bombers. The manned plane is essential in search and rescue, transport, evacuation of wounded troops, and other missions where the human factor is decisive.

In the 1970s, both the Soviet Union and the United States developed high-performance, complex airplanes for manned flight. The Soviet MiG-25 Foxbat attack and fighter plane could fly up to Mach 3 in short bursts and was capable of firing the air-to-air Acrid missile. The United States developed the McDonnell Douglas F-15 Eagle, an effective long-range flier that carried Sparrow and Sidewinder missiles.

OTHER SPECIALIZED AND MULTIROLE AIRCRAFT

Among other specialized manned planes designed in the postwar era have been the short-takeoff-and-landing (STOL) and vertical-takeoff-and-landing (VTOL) crafts. The Korean and Vietnam wars proved the need for planes able to take off and land in remote jungles, forested areas, and on ships. The STOL and VTOL craft provided some independence from long permanent runways. Typical of these craft is the Swedish Saab SF-37 Viggen and the British Hawker-Siddeley Sea Harrier.

The high production cost of specialized aircraft has led to the growing use of the multirole combat aircraft (MRCA). The MRCA is an airplane that can be adapted to a variety

A Panavia Tornado of the Royal Air Force. © AP Images

of functions—bomber, fighter, and reconnaissance. An example is the European-made Panavia Tornado, commissioned by Britain, West Germany, and Italy, and made operational in 1976. The Tornado carries up to 18,000 pounds (8,200 kilograms) of bombs, missiles, and a mix of laser, radar, and electronic aids. A next-generation MRCA, the Lockheed Martin F-35 Lightning (or Joint Strike Fighter), was undergoing advanced flight testing in the early 21st century; it had variant models that were capable of STOL and carrier-based landing.

UNMANNED AERIAL VEHICLES

A little-known but important milestone in modern warfare was reached in 2009: in that year the United States Air Force trained more operators of unmanned aerial vehicles (UAVs) than it did pilots. In an age when war is increasingly dominated by robots, the U.S. military alone fields at least 7,000 of these machines, which are either remotely guided by a human using a radio link or self-guided by preprogrammed flight plans. Interest in UAVs is global, however. More than 60 manufacturers in at least 40 countries are now servicing a market that is expected to exceed tens of billions of dollars by 2020. It is not surprising, then, that Quentin Davies, the U.K.'s minister for defense equipment and support, predicted in July 2009 that the world is now witnessing the last generation of manned combat aircraft and that by 2030 UAVs will have displaced them.

UAVs, also called remotely piloted vehicles (RPVs) or unmanned aircraft systems (UASs), are aircraft without a pilot onboard.

Fixed-wing UAVs resemble "smart weapons" such as cruise missiles, but they are superior because they return to their base after a mission and can be reused. Also, UAVs have two decisive advantages over manned aircraft: their use does not risk the lives of aircrews, and they can loiter over areas of interest longer than most types of aircraft with human pilots. The current generation of UAVs varies in size from small propeller-driven hand-launched models such as the German army's Aladin to jet-powered intercontinental-range craft such as the U.S. Air Force's RQ-4 Global Hawk.

The earliest UAVs were known as remotely piloted vehicles (RPVs), or drones. Drones were small radio-controlled aircraft first used during World War II as targets for fighters and antiaircraft guns. Truly modern UAVs did not begin to appear over battlefields until the 1980s, when a number of technical advancements made them much more effective. Advanced composite materials made for lighter, stronger airframes, and improved electronics permitted the development of high-resolution TV and infrared cameras. Also, full implementation of the Global Positioning System (GPS) in the 1990s made it possible to navigate UAVs with a precision that was previously unattainable.

UAVs began to garner media attention during NATO's intervention in the Yugoslav civil war of the 1990s. In 1995, the United States Air Force put the RQ-1 Predator into service for airborne surveillance and target acquisition. With its pusher propeller driven by a four-cylinder gasoline engine, the Predator could cruise at 87 miles (140 kilometers) per hour, stay aloft for up to 16 hours, and reach altitudes of 25,000 feet (7,600 meters). Predators flying over Yugoslavia tracked troop movements, monitored refugees, and marked targets so that manned aircraft could attack them with laser-guided bombs.

The Predator remains the most widely used battlefield UAV operated by the United States. The entire system consists of the vehicle itself (with built-in radar, TV and infrared cameras, and laser designator), a ground-control station, and a communication suite to link the two by satellite. Though pilotless, the Predator is operated by approximately 55 personnel, including a pilot operator and a sensor operator as well as intelligence, maintenance, and launch and

The camera of an MQ-9 Reaper showing a truck in the heads-up display of a pilot in a ground control station during a training mission. Ethan Miller/Getty Images

recovery specialists. The current version, designated the MQ-1, went into service in 2001 armed with two laser-guided AGM-114 Hellfire missiles, giving the UAV the ability to attack targets as well as identify them. A turboprop-powered version of the Predator, called the

MQ-9 Reaper, is significantly larger and has a greater payload. The Reaper has been operational since 2007 with U.S. forces and is also used by Britain's Royal Air Force.

The next wave of UAV development is likely to be so-called uninhabited combat air vehicles (UCAVs). If the experimental Boeing X-45 and Northrop Grumman X-47 are representative of these vehicles, they will resemble small B-2 Spirit stealth bombers and will vary in size from one-third to one-sixth the gross weight of a single-seat fighter-bomber. They will most likely supplement or even replace piloted fighter-bombers in the attack role in high-threat environments. Finally, large, extremely light solar-powered "endurance UAVs" have been flown in order to test the feasibility of communications and surveillance vehicles that would stay on station at high altitude for months or even years at a time.

THE AFGHANISTAN WAR

After the Sept. 11, 2001, attacks on New York and Washington, D.C., the United States embarked on its first war of the 21st century. The remote, mountainous terrain of Afghanistan and the nature of the Taliban and al-Qaeda's military power negated many of the technological advantages boasted by the U.S. and its NATO allies—supersonic air superiority fighters were of limited use against an enemy that lacked an air force, and stealth was redundant when there was little in the way of an integrated air defense network. Instead, one the most important elements of U.S. air power was its airlift capability, which allowed it to carry men and materiel some 7,000 miles (11,000 kilometers) from the continental United States to installations such as Bagram Airfield, a base just north of the Afghan capital of Kabul. As the war dragged on and coalition casualties grew, airborne medical evacuation increased in importance. Seriously wounded soldiers were transported by air to U.S. bases in Europe for treatment that was not available in Afghanistan.

Close air support was another critical mission for the United States Air Force in Afghanistan, with workhorses such as the A-10 Warthog providing decisive firepower for troops on the ground. Although its Cold War design was originally intended to combat Soviet armor, the A-10's intimidating 30mm Gatling gun and its durable airframe combined to make it the premier ground attack platform in the Afghan theatre. Perhaps the most notable advance in air power in the Afghanistan War, however, was the widespread use of UAVs. Strikes by armed drones were credited with killing numerous high-value targets, although the legality of such attacks—especially when they targeted American citizens—was questioned by some.

THE IRAQ WAR

Air power played a significant role in the first Persian Gulf War, and U.S. aircraft remained a presence in Iraqi skies in subsequent years. Allied planes enforced "no-fly zones" in northern and southern Iraq to prevent Iraqi aircraft from harassing opponents to Saddām Hussein's regime. The most conspicuous use of allied air power in the interwar years was Operation Desert Fox, a U.S. air attack on Iraqi military installations in 1998 that was designed to compel Iraqi officials to comply with a UN weapons inspection program.

Weapons inspection remained a contentious issue into the 21st century, and U.S.

Fires blazing on the west bank of the Tigris River after the United States began its "shock and awe" bombing campaign on Baghdad in the opening days of the Iraq War. **Mirrorpix/Getty Images**

Pres. George W. Bush made the case for war based on the claim that Iraq possessed weapons of mass destruction. The U.S.-led invasion began in March 2003 with a massive air attack that targeted government and military facilities. The scale of the bombing campaign was intended to cause "shock and awe" among both the Iraqi leadership and the rank and file of the military, and it might have contributed to the disorganized and largely ineffective Iraqi resistance in the opening weeks of the war. In addition, the so-called "light footprint" invasion strategy was meant to exploit the overwhelming U.S. advantage in training and technology, using special forces units and air power in the place of hundreds of thousands of infantry troops.

While this proved adequate in the conventionally fought early part of the conflict, commanders needed to find new ways to utilize air power as a counterinsurgency tool. Air strikes in densely populated cities carried far too much risk of civilian casualties, and they were wholly ineffective against the improvised explosive devices that were the major threat to coalition troops. In the later years of the war, the threat of air power, embodied by low-level flyovers by coalition aircraft, proved to be an effective negotiating tool for ground commanders.

CHAPTER 6

MAJOR AIR FORCES OF THE WORLD

F ew nations had air forces prior to World War I. In the early 21st century, more than 130 nations had established air forces. These ranged from the powerful military organizations of the United States, Great Britain, and China—each with hundreds of thousands of members and thousands of aircraft—to such tiny groups as the air force of the Republic of Benin, which had several dozen men operating a handful of aircraft.

There are two methods of staffing an air force. In some countries, such as the United States, Canada, and Japan, the air force relies on volunteers who enlist for a specific number of years. In other nations, such as Germany and Israel, young people are drafted into military service. In terms of size, strength, advanced technology, and combat readiness, the two leading air forces for most of the late 20th century were those of the Soviet Union and the United States, with the United States Air Force leading in the early part of the 21st century.

CHINA

The People's Liberation Army Air Force (PLAAF) was established in 1949, in the closing months of the Chinese Civil War. From its inception, the PLAAF relied heavily on Soviet assistance for both aircraft and training, and within a year of its creation, the PLAAF received its baptism by fire in the skies over Korea. Although the MiG-15 used by Russian, Chinese, and North Korean forces was, in many ways, a superior aircraft to the U.S. F-86 Sabre, Chinese pilots were consistently bested by their American counterparts, owing largely to the caliber of the United States Air Force training regimen. The PLAAF was again tested during the Second Taiwan Strait Crisis. Over several months in 1958, Chinese MiG fighters sparred with Taiwanese F-86s. These contests overwhelmingly favored the Taiwanese, who had access to Sidewinder heat-seeking air-to-air missiles.

The PLAAF overcame these early setbacks, and improved air defense systems served as a check on Taiwanese probes of the mainland. As relations with Russia worsened in the 1960s and '70s, however, China's primary source of new aircraft vanished, and the

The Bayi Aerobatics Team, a demonstration team of the PLAAF, performing during an air show in northeast China. AFP/Getty Images

PLAAF attempted to make do with outdated technology. The collapse of the Soviet Union in 1991 led to an influx of advanced aircraft, as Russia sought to raise funds and divest itself of surplus hardware. In the early 21st century, the PLAAF was a 300,000-strong force with some 1,600 combat-ready aircraft. The bulk of the PLAAF's fighter fleet was derived from or directly based on Russian designs such as the MiG-21.

China's domestic aircraft industry remained in its infancy, and many "new" Chinese designs bore a striking resemblance to American planes such as the F-22 and the F-35. These facts, along with a series of hacking incidents that targeted American defense companies, led many analysts to assume that Chinese aerospace research was being conducted via cyberespionage.

ENGLAND

The first air units in Britain's military were formed eight years after the first powered flight took place in 1903. In April 1911, an air battalion of the Royal Engineers was formed, consisting of one balloon and one airplane company. In December 1911, the

British Admiralty formed the first naval flying school, at the Royal Aero Club ground at Eastchurch, Kent.

In May 1912, a combined Royal Flying Corps (RFC) was formed with naval and military wings and a Central Flying School at Upavon on Salisbury Plain. The specialized aviation requirements of the navy made it appear, however, that separate organization was desirable, and on July 1, 1914, the naval wing of the RFC became the Royal Naval Air Service (RNAS), the military wing retaining the title Royal Flying Corps.

On the outbreak of World War I in August 1914, the RFC, possessing a total of 179 airplanes, sent four squadrons to France. On April 1, 1918, the RNAS and RFC were absorbed into the Royal Air Force (RAF), which took its place beside the British navy and army as a separate service with its own ministry under a secretary of state for air. The strength of the RAF in November 1918 was nearly 291,000 officers and airmen. It possessed 200 operational squadrons and nearly the same number of training squadrons, with a total of 22,647 aircraft.

To train permanent officers for the flying branch of the RAF, a cadet college was established at Cranwell, Lincolnshire, in 1920. The RAF staff college was opened in 1922 at Andover, Hampshire.

At the outbreak of World War II in September 1939, the first-line strength of the RAF in the United Kingdom was about 2,000 aircraft. The RAF fighter pilots, however, distinguished themselves during the Battle of Britain in the early stages of the war against the numerically superior German Luftwaffe. By the time the war ended, the strength of the RAF was 963,000 personnel. When the wartime forces were demobilized in 1945, however, the total strength of the RAF was reduced to about 150,000, the approximate number retained into the 1980s. That number had dropped significantly by the early 21st century, as part of an overall force reduction strategy implemented by the British military. With 40,000 troops and just over 300 combat-ready aircraft, the RAF was a smaller, more focused, force than it had been in previous years. Despite its reduced size, the RAF remained a potent instrument for projecting British force across the globe, as demonstrated in the wars in Afghanistan and Iraq, as well as the NATO air campaign in Libya.

GERMANY

The Luftwaffe was formally created in 1935, but military aviation had existed in the shadows in Germany since the end of World War I. The Treaty of Versailles had banned Germany from possessing warplanes, so much of the groundwork for the Luftwaffe was laid by civilian aircraft production and Freikorps units (private paramilitary groups). By the beginning of World War II, the Luftwaffe was arguably the best air force in the world, and its robust role within the combined arms strategy utilized by German military planners allowed for the use of blitzkreig tactics against outclassed Allied armies. The structure of the Luftwaffe very much reflected the whims of its commander, Hermann Göring, and over 3 million men served in air force, air defense, and paratrooper units from 1939 to 1945. This incarnation of the Luftwaffe was disbanded by victorious Allied powers in 1946.

The service was reconstituted in 1956 as an integral part of the NATO defense network in central Europe. Outfitted primarily with American aircraft, West German pilots also received flight training in the United States. While this demonstrated the strength of the relationship between the two countries, it was also rooted in practicality, as locations such as Holloman Air Force Base in New Mexico boasted more airspace and better consistent flying weather than could be found in Germany.

With the reuniting of Germany and the fading of Cold War threats, the modern Luftwaffe is focused primarily on its role within the European Union's defense structure. With more than 40,000 troops and some 300 combat-capable aircraft, Luftwaffe participation in NATO missions in Kosovo and Afghanistan demonstrated that German air power remained a potent force. With the maturation of Germany's domestic aerospace industry, the reliance on American technology was eased, and the Eurofighter Typhoon, a multirole attack aircraft built by the European Aeronautic Defence and Space (EADS) consortium, served as the Luftwaffe's principal combat aircraft in the 21st century.

ISRAEL

The Israeli Air Force (IAF) was formed in 1948, just weeks after Israel's declaration of independence. Its roots were in the air wing of the Haganah, the Zionist military organization that served as a Jewish defense force in the decades before the establishment of Israel. The young air force, which was bolstered by foreign volunteer pilots as well as clandestine support from the Soviet Union by way of Czechoslovakia, was of crucial importance in the first Arab-Israeli War. With a relatively small area to defend, and surrounded by hostile and numerically superior neighbours, Israeli military planners recognized that speed and the ability to strike deep into enemy territory would be crucial elements in the young country's defense doctrine. To that end, the IAF was given a central role in subsequent military conflicts.

In the Six Day War (June 5–10, 1967), the IAF demonstrated absolute command of the skies, downing six Syrian fighters and destroying Egypt's air force on the ground in an attack that was as successful as it was audacious. Such strikes came to be regarded as the norm for the IAF, as evidenced by Operation Opera, a June 1981 air raid that destroyed an Iraqi nuclear reactor and effectively curbed that country's nuclear ambitions indefinitely. The IAF was often dispatched to

A drone of the IAF preparing to land at the Palmachim Air Force Base in Israel. Gali Tibbon/AFP/Getty Images

respond to rocket and mortar attacks from Lebanon, Syria, and Palestinian-controlled territories. In the early 21st century, the IAF numbered some 34,000 troops, and its more than 500 combat-ready aircraft included F-15s and F-16s, as well as AH-1 Cobra and AH-64 Apache attack helicopters. Israel also boasted one of the most advanced UAV fleets in the world, and it ranked among the world's largest exporters of drone technology. In addition, the IAF held more than 200 fighters and ground-attack aircraft in a ready reserve.

North Korea

North Korean Pres. Kim Il-sung established the Korean People's Army Air Force (KPAAF) on Aug. 20, 1947, and it became a separate branch of the armed forces the following year. Its mettle was soon tested when war broke out on the Korean peninsula, as North Korean armies invaded the South on June 25, 1950. The Soviet Union supplied planes and pilots to the North Korean war effort, and the arrival of the MiG-15 jet fighter in the skies over Korea marked a turning point in the history of air combat. The U.S. rushed into production the F-86 Sabre, and the age of jet warfare began, as North Korean, Soviet, and Chinese pilots took to the skies in an area that would become known as "MiG Alley." Despite the initial shock, the UN forces quickly regained air superiority, an advantage they would maintain for the duration of the war.

While open hostilities were concluded in July 1953, North Korea and South Korea technically remained at war, as peace negotiations between the two parties were never officially concluded. This set the tone for North Korea's defense posture, which remained assertive and, at times, belligerent. Its air force received extensive technical and material support from the Soviets throughout the Cold War, but this largely evaporated with the demise of the Soviet Union. Thus, in the 21st century, the KPAAF was a large, if hollow, institution. Although it boasted more than 100,000 troops, its equipment was largely obsolete. Of the hundreds of fighter aircraft in its inventory, only a few dozen were modern MiG-29s, and the combat readiness of those craft was questionable due to shortages of replacement parts. In addition, chronic fuel shortages in North Korea meant that pilots received as little as 20 hours a year of flight training.

THE SOVIET UNION AND RUSSIA

Soviet military aviation dated from late 1917, when the Bolsheviks organized the Workers and Peasants Air Fleet that later became the Red Air Force and, still later, the VVS. It was reorganized in 1924. The Soviet air force had three main elements integrated under a general staff—the VVS, the Strategic Rocket Forces (RSVN), and the Air Defense Forces (PVO). The three operating sections of the VVS were Frontal Aviation, which provided tactical support; Long-Range Aviation, the strategic bomber force; and Military Transport Aviation. A fourth element, Naval Aviation, was not directly responsible to the general staff. Each command consisted of divisions of three or more regiments, which, in turn, contained three squadrons of 12 aircraft each.

The estimated 475,000 members of the Soviet air force were supplemented by some 950,000 reserves and 550,000 members of the national air defense. The Soviets maintained at least 500 air bases, including 100 in the Arctic and subarctic regions. Their air forces were deployed in the Soviet Union and in eastern Germany (the former German Democratic Republic), Hungary, Poland, and Czechoslovakia.

Soviet aircraft included MiG fighters and interceptors, Tupolev Tu-26 bombers, Bison refuelers, and Sukhoi Su-7b Fitter-A ground attack aircraft. In addition, they controlled a wide-ranging missile system that included

A Soyuz spacecraft launching from the Baikonur space center, a Russian base, in Kazakhstan. Bill Ingalls/NASA/Getty Images

AIR FORCES IN OUTER SPACE

The nations of the world have been reaching into outer space since the development of jet and rocket propulsion in the late 1940s. In 1956, the United States Air Force launched the Bell X-2, a rocket-powered research craft, to an altitude of nearly 24 miles (39 kilometers). On Oct. 4, 1957, the Space Age began in earnest as the Soviet Union used an intercontinental ballistic missile to launch the 184-pound (83-kilogram) *Sputnik* satellite into orbit.

By the early 1980s, in both the Soviet Union and the United States, satellites that could use laser beams and particle beams to destroy ground-based targets and spacecraft were under study. Orbital bombardment weapons were also under study. The Soviets researched the SS-9 Scarp, a satellite armed with a nuclear warhead, which would remain in orbit until needed.

The ability of space vehicles to gather intelligence has grown. Early reconnaissance satellites furnished detailed pictures of military installations, either by television or by photographic film returned to Earth in reentry capsules. Others eavesdropped on electronic conversations. Reconnaissance satellites carrying infrared sensors can also detect missile launchings or heat-producing craft. However, by the early 1990s, the United States and other nations moved away from developing these military devices as part of a far-reaching pledge to reduce their arsenals; indeed, the Navstar Global Positioning System, a U.S.

Department of Defense project, was made available for civilian use in a move that revolutionized terrestrial navigation. In 2007, China successfully destroyed one of its own defunct satellites with a ground-based missile, an exercise that was seen by analysts as a demonstration of China's anti-satellite capabilities.

The Soviet Union first launched a military observation satellite, the *Kosmos 112*, in 1969 to provide coverage of Norway, Alaska, and Greenland. Vela satellites can orbit some 70,000 miles (113,000 kilometers) from Earth to monitor nuclear explosions in space.

more than 12,000 surface-to-air missiles and 1,500 intercontinental ballistic missiles.

After the dissolution of the Soviet Union in 1991, defense policy was devolved to the newly independent countries, but Russia maintained numerous bases in former Soviet republics. Most notable among these was the Baikonur space center in Kazakhstan, which had functioned as the base of the Soviet space program (it was scheduled to be replaced by a new launch site in the Russian Far East by 2020).

Although a fraction of its size the Soviet era and further reduced by budgetary constraints in the 21st century, the Russian Air Force remained one of the largest military air forces in the world. With some 150,000 troops and more than 1,600 combat-ready aircraft, its effectiveness was buoyed by a long tradition of domestic research and development. The Sukhoi T-50 represented the next stage in Russian fighter technology. Designed as a stealthy, multirole attack craft, the T-50 (or PAK-FA, a name derived from the Russian acronym for the project) was widely seen as the Russian counterpart to the American F-22 Raptor.

THE UNITED STATES AIR FORCE

The Air Force has been a separate branch of the United States armed services only since 1947. Before that time it was part of the Army. The first air arm was established in 1907 as the Aeronautical Division of the Army Signal Corps. The First Aero Squadron was organized in 1914. It served with the Mexican Border Expedition in 1916.

The three components of the United States Department of Defense are the departments of the Air Force, the Army, and the Navy. The Department of the Air Force is headed by a civilian secretary, who is appointed by the president of the United States. At the head of the Air Force's entire military staff is the chief of staff who is also appointed by the president. Together with the chiefs of staff of the Army and the Navy, he is a member of the Joint Chiefs of Staff, who serve as the principal military advisers to the president and to the secretary of defense.

MAJOR COMMANDS

The operation of the Air Force is divided into ten major commands, each of which is responsible for a specific area of the Air Force's mission.

Air Combat Command (ACC) was established in June 1992 from elements of the former Strategic Air Command and the Tactical Air Command. ACC is responsible for a force of fighters, bombers, reconnaissance aircraft, combat delivery aircraft, electronic warfare aircraft, air rescue aircraft, and command, control, communications, and intelligence aircraft. In wartime ACC provides air forces to the United States military's Unified Combatant Commands. ACC also supplies air defense forces to the North American Aerospace Defense Command (NORAD).

ACC's headquarters are at Joint Base Langley-Eustis, in Norfolk, Va. ACC is made up of three numbered air forces—the 1st, at Tyndall AFB, near Panama City, Fla.; the 9th, at Shaw AFB, near Sumter, S.C.; and the 12th, at Davis-Monthan AFB, near Tucson, Ariz. The United States Air

An F-22 Raptor being prepared for taxiing at Joint Base Langley-Eustis, the headquarters of the ACC. **U.S. Air Force photo/ Airman 1st Class Teresa Zimmerman**

Force Air Warfare Center at Eglin AFB in Florida and the United States Air Force Warfare Center at Nellis AFB in Nevada are also under the control of ACC.

Air Mobility Command (ΛMC), head-quartered at Scott AFB, near Belleville, Ill., is responsible for the air transport of United States troops and supplies during wartime. Formed in June 1992 from the

PARARESCUERS

United States Air Force Pararescue Jumpers (PJs) are an elite force of combat medics who have been trained to deploy via air, land, or sea to treat the seriously wounded and to conduct rescue and recovery operations. Their mission extends to both military and civilians, and they are regarded as some of the most skilled and versatile emergency medical specialists in the U.S. armed forces. The unit has its origins in the Burma theatre in World War II, when a pair of medical corpsmen were parachuted into the jungle to aid with the recovery of more than 20 people who had bailed out of a disabled transport aircraft. Pararescuers served with distinction throughout the Vietnam War, and

Members of the Air Force pararescue team descending from a helicopter to meet a team member near the wreckage site of a missing warplane. © AP Images

one, Airman William H. Pitsenbarger, was awarded the Medal of Honor for gallantry. PJs also played a significant role in the extraction of injured personnel during the "Blackhawk Down" incident in Mogadishu, Somalia, and were of critical importance in the Afghanistan War, where the remote and mountainous terrain made insertion and extraction of personnel by land a time-consuming and daunting effort. Prospective pararescuers undergo a year of preparation and training in survival techniques, basic and advanced parachuting, combat diving, and emergency medicine. These serve as a prelude to a six-month pararescue course, the completion of which entitles graduates to wear the group's distinctive maroon beret.

former Military Aircraft Command and elements of SAC, AMC also provides aerial refueling for America's combat aircraft.

Air Force Materiel Command (AFMC), at Wright-Patterson AFB, near Dayton, Ohio, was created in July 1992 through the combination of the Air Force Logistics Command and the Air Force Systems Command. AFMC procures, stores, distributes, and provides maintenance for the Air Force's aircraft, missiles, munitions, and other supplies. AFMC also handles the research, development, and testing of satellites, boosters, and space probes for the Department of Defense.

Air Force Space Command (AFSPACECOM), at Peterson AFB, Colorado Springs, Colo., provides strategic aerospace defense through management of the nation's military satellites and ground-radar systems. AFSPACECOM also controls America's force of intercontinental ballistic missiles (ICBMs). Two numbered air forces—the 14th, at Vandenberg AFB, near Lompac, Calif., and the 24th, at Lackland AFB, Tex., and at Robins Air Force Base, Ga.—are part of AFSPACECOM.

Air Force Special Operations Command (AFSOC) is headquartered at Hurlburt Field, near Fort Walton Beach, Fla. Its forces specialize in using helicopters and gunships for a variety of special operations. These include counterterrorism, psychological operations, special reconnaissance, unconventional warfare, personnel recovery, and counternarcotics.

Air Education and Training Command (AETC) operates out of Joint Base San Antonio Randolph, near San Antonio, Tex. It is responsible for the recruitment and training of airmen and officers. Its educational programs include the Air University, headquartered at Maxwell AFB, near Montgomery, Ala. AETC includes the 2nd Air Force, headquartered at Keesler AFB, near Biloxi, Miss.

Air Force Reserve Command (AFRC) is located at Robins Air Force Base, near Macon, Ga. It ensures that the Air Force maintains sufficient active-duty personnel by mobilizing reserves as needed. Three numbered air forces—the 4th at March Air Reserve Base near Riverside, Calif.; the 10th, at Joint Reserve Base, Fort Worth, Tex.; and the 22nd, at Dobbins Air Reserve Base near Marietta, Ga.—are under its command. The AFRC's 53rd Weather Reconnaissance Squadron, out of Keesler Air Force Base in Biloxi, Miss., monitors hurricanes for the National Weather Service.

Air Force Global Strike Command (AFGSC) oversees the Air Force's nuclear deterrence capabilities, represented by three intercontinental ballistic missile wings, two B-52 wings, and a B-2 Spirit wing. It is based at Barksdale AFB, outside Shreveport, La. It commands two numbered air forces: the 8th, at Barksdale AFB and the 20th, at F.E. Warren AFB, outside Cheyenne, Wyo.

United States Air Forces in Europe Air Forces Africa (USAFE-AFAFRICA) is headquartered at Ramstein Air Base, Germany. USAFE-AFAFRICA is responsible for Air Force operations in the U.S. European Command and U.S. Africa Command. Its numbered air force is the 3rd Air Force, based at Ramstein.

Pacific Air Forces (PACAF) is based at Joint Base Pearl Harbor-Hickam, in Oahu, Hawaii. PACAF is responsible for Air Force operations in the Pacific Command. Its units include the 5th Air Force, at Yokota Air Base, in Japan; the 7th Air Force, at Osan Air Base, in South Korea; and the 11th Air Force, at Joint Base Elmendorf-Richardson, near Anchorage, Alaska.

In addition to the ten major commands, the Air Force relies on many separate operating agencies, which perform specialized support, logistical, or administrative functions that are relatively narrow in scope.

AIRCRAFT

The Air Force has had a variety of aircraft at its disposal over the course of its history. The following are some of those in use in the 21st century.

F-16 Fighting Falcon

The design of the F-16 dates to the 1970s, but its versatility and its proven combat effectiveness ensured that it remained the backbone of the USAF's fighter fleet into the 21st century. The single-seat, single-engine craft could be configured with a variety of weapons loadouts, it could travel at Mach 2, and its relatively low cost (less than $20 million each) made it a popular choice for the export market.

F-22 Raptor

The F-22 was designed to replace the aging F-15 as the USAF's premier air superiority fighter. However, dramatic cost overruns and production delays meant that the world's most advanced and expensive fighter jet—priced at an estimated $400 million each—never fully lived up to expectations. Its stealth capabilities and unmatched handling in the air were wasted on enemies that lacked air forces, and lingering safety and maintenance issues led the Pentagon to redirect its efforts to the more versatile F-35 Joint Strike Fighter. Of the 650 F-22s that were initially planned, fewer than 200 were actually produced.

A-10 Thunderbolt II

Nicknamed the "Warthog," the A-10 is perhaps the most effective fixed-wing close-air support platform in the world. Possessing the maneuverability and durability to operate at low speed and at low altitude, the A-10 bristles with ordnance, but it is best known for its nose-mounted 30mm Gatling cannon. Redundant and manual backup flight systems improve the craft's survivability in combat, and the cockpit features a titanium "bathtub" design that shields the pilot from ground fire. Its ability to operate in rugged conditions made it ideally suited for combat in the mountainous terrain of Afghanistan.

MQ-1 Predator

Arguably the best-known UAV in the United States Air Force's remotely piloted fleet, the Predator was designed as a reconnaissance craft, but the addition of Hellfire missiles in 2001 added the term "drone strike" to the defense lexicon. Although less heavily armed than the MQ-9 Reaper, the Predator's ability to loiter on target for up to 24 hours and the complete removal

AIR FORCE ONE

Air Force One is any aircraft of the United States Air Force that is carrying the president of the United States. Strictly speaking, Air Force One is the radio call sign adopted by any Air Force plane while the president is aboard. In common parlance, however, the call sign has become identified with specific aircraft reserved for use by the president for travel within the United States or abroad. Since 1991, two such aircraft

One of the two aircraft that currently serve as Air Force One.
Johannes Eisele/AFP/Getty Images

have been in service: identical Boeing 747-200B jumbo jets bearing the tail numbers 28000 and 29000 and the Air Force designation VC-25A.

Each of the current Air Force One aircraft is equipped with classified security and defense systems, including measures to protect onboard electronics against the electromagnetic pulse of a nuclear explosion. A telecommunications center is located in the upper level, and in the lower level is a cargo hold with a self-contained baggage-handling system. The middle level contains accommodations for as many as 70 passengers in addition to the crew of 26. These accommodations include seating and work areas for media representatives, security staff, and other personnel; a combination conference-dining room; an in-flight pharmacy and emergency medical equipment; and two galleys in which as many as 100 servings per meal can be prepared. The presidential suite, located in the quiet forward area of the plane, contains an office, a bedroom, and a lavatory.

The two jets have a range of almost 8,000 miles (more than 12,000 km) unrefueled, but with in-flight refueling they are capable of circling the globe. They are based at Andrews Air Force Base in Maryland, near Washington, D.C., and are assigned to the 89th Airlift Wing of the Air Force's Air Mobility Command. They have served presidents, vice presidents (at which time they are known as Air Force Two), and other dignitaries under the administrations of George H.W. Bush, Bill Clinton, George W. Bush, and Barack Obama. The pair of jets is slated for replacement by three new aircraft between 2017 and 2021.

of its operator from harm's way made it a valuable addition to the U.S. arsenal.

C-130

The Lockheed Martin C-130 Hercules was an unconventional multirole aircraft. In its standard configuration, it was a rugged turboprop-driven transport plane. The standard C-130 could be tailored in a wide variety of ways; it could also serve as an airborne refucling platform, a firefighting plane, an airborne hospital, and an electronic warfare and special operations support craft. The AC-130 was probably the best known of the C-130 variants, however. Boasting a 25mm autocannon, a 40mm cannon, and a 105mm howitzer, the AC-130 could loiter over a battlefield, providing an incredible volume of fire in support of troops below.

CHAPTER 8

HISTORY OF THE UNITED STATES AIR FORCE

U.S. military activities in the air began with the use of balloons by the army for reconnaissance during the American Civil War and the Spanish-American War. The Aeronautical Division of the Signal Corps of the U.S. Army was created on Aug. 1, 1907. Congress passed the first appropriations for aeronautics in 1911 and on July 18, 1914, created the Aviation Section of the Signal Corps.

WORLD WAR I

The first use of military aircraft, in an action against Pancho Villa in Mexico in 1916, was a failure. The next year the United States entered World War I with one ill-equipped air unit, the 1st Aero Squadron. The Appropriations Act of July 24, 1917, provided increased funds, and an executive order of May 20, 1918, removed aviation from the Signal Corps by establishing the U.S. Army Air Service. By

Hydrogen gas generator being used to inflate an observation balloon during the American Civil War, 1862. U.S. Department of Defense; Brady Collection

war's end, the Air Service had attained a strength of 195,000 officers and men and had organized 45 squadrons with a complement of 740 planes. Until the later stages of the war, U.S. squadrons in France were equipped mainly with British and French planes. Much of the success of U.S. military air activity during World War I was attributable to Brigadier General William ("Billy") Mitchell, a combat air commander who directed U.S. air attacks of increasing strength up to the war's end.

After World War I, the Air Service was quickly reduced to a tiny fraction of its former strength. Mitchell became a forceful exponent of the movement to create a separate air force on a par with the Army and Navy. Despite his efforts, however, the Army Reorganization Act of 1920 created the Air Service as a combatant unit within the Army. The Air Corps Act of 1926 replaced the Air Service with the Army Air Corps, which was responsible for the training and logistical support of its units, while the tactical units themselves were under the control of Army commands.

WORLD WAR II

On the eve of World War II, in September 1939, the Army's air arm had a strength of 24,000 officers and men and about 1,500 tactical planes. In 1940, however, the Air Corps began a rapid expansion in response to events in Europe. The Air Corps was supplanted on June 20, 1941, by the Army Air Forces as an autonomous command within the Army, and in March 1942, after American entry into the

WOMEN AIRFORCE SERVICE PILOTS

The Women Airforce Service Pilots (WASP) had its origins with a pair of exceptionally skilled and ambitious female pilots. Prior to U.S. entry into World War II, Nancy Harkness Love, the youngest American woman to have earned her private pilot's license until that time, had lobbied for the creation of a program that would allow female pilots to ferry warplanes from factories to air bases. At the same time, Jackie Cochran, one of the most accomplished pilots of her era, demonstrated the feasibility of such an idea by flying a Lend-Lease bomber to England and organizing a group of female

Four WASP pilots leaving a B-17 Fortress plane at the training school at Lockbourne Air Force Base near Columbus, Ohio.
PhotoQuest/Archive Photos/Getty Images

pilots for war transport service as part of the British Air Transport Auxiliary. By 1942, as the war reduced the number of qualified male pilots available for transport duty, American military leaders became increasingly receptive to Love and Cochran's ideas.

In September 1942, Love organized the Women's Auxiliary Ferrying Squadron (WAFS), and more than two dozen of the country's best female civilian pilots were soon reporting to New Castle Army Air Base in Delaware for transport training. Two months later, Cochran convinced Army Air Forces commander Hap Arnold to activate the Women's Flying Training Detachment (WFTD), a similar program based at Howard Hughes Airport in Houston. The two programs operated separately until August 1943, when they were merged as the WASP, with Cochran taking the role as director. More than 25,000 women applied to serve in the WASP, although fewer than 10 percent of that number were accepted. Candidates had to be between 21 and 35 years old, possess a commercial pilot's license, and have the physical endurance to complete the military training regimen that was part of the selection process. The women of the WASP logged more than 60 million miles in the air and flew every type of aircraft in the Army Air Forces. Unlike the Women's Army Corps (WAC) or the Women Accepted for Volunteer Emergency Service (WAVES), the WASP were considered part of the civil service and were not militarized as an official auxiliary force. Thus, the 38 women who were killed while serving in the WASP were not entitled to burial expenses or survivor's benefits. The WASP were finally militarized in 1977, an act that made official the veteran status of those who had served.

war, all Army air units were merged into the Army Air Forces (AAF) under a single commander, General Henry H. Arnold. From its headquarters in Washington, D.C., the AAF directed the expansion of the air arm into a powerful organization composed of 16 air forces (12 of them overseas), 243 combat groups, 2,400,000 officers and men, and nearly 80,000 aircraft.

During the war, two U.S. air forces—the 8th and the 15th—participated with the Royal Air Force Bomber Command in the strategic bombing of Germany. Two other air forces—the 9th and 12th—supplied the U.S. air cooperation needed in the victorious ground campaigns in North Africa, Sicily, Italy, and Western Europe. In the Pacific theatre, the 5th, 7th, and 13th air forces joined with the Army and Navy in the series of island conquests that were stepping-stones to the conquest of Japan. On the Asian mainland, the 10th Air Force in the China-Burma-India theatre and the 14th in China supported British and Chinese armies against the Japanese. From the Mariana Islands, B-29 bombers of the 20th Air Force carried out the bombing campaign of Japan that culminated in the dropping of atomic bombs on Hiroshima and Nagasaki.

POSTWAR PERIOD AND COLD WAR

The swift demobilization of the postwar period sharply reduced the strength of the AAF to about 300,000 officers and men by June 1947. The need for a separate air arm of the U.S. military had become clear by this time, however, and in anticipation of this, the AAF was reorganized in March 1946 along lines that emphasized functions rather than geographical areas. The basic pattern of unit organization, in descending order, was established as follows: command, air force, air division, wing, group, squadron, and flight. On July 26, 1947, the National Security Act created the independent U.S. Air Force. The National Security Act Amendments of 1949 reorganized the military services, with the Department of the Air Force included within the Department of Defense.

The advent of nuclear weapons delivered by long-range bombers meant that the Air Force would play a decisive role in any future superpower conflict during the Cold War. To this end, the Strategic Air Command (SAC) was created in 1946 to launch nuclear-armed bombers from bases in the United States and elsewhere. In 1956, SAC was also made responsible for the United States' intermediate and long-range ballistic missiles. Thus, until its abolition in 1992, after the end of the Cold War, SAC played the leading role in the United States' nuclear deterrent forces. Conventional American air power played an important support role in both the Korean (1950–53) and Vietnam (1965–75) wars and was the decisive factor in the Allied victory over Iraq in the Persian Gulf War (1991).

INTO THE 21ST CENTURY

The United States Air Force was by far the largest and most technologically advanced air force in the world in the early 21st century. Developments in stealth technology saw the debut of the first true stealth fighter, the F-22 Raptor, which was capable of reaching supersonic speeds without the use of afterburners. Cold War–era platforms such as the F-15 and F-16 found renewed life with enhanced avionics, electronic warfare, and weapons systems, and the venerable B-52 entered its seventh decade of service. The expansion of the Air Force's drone

An MQ-9 Reaper, one of the drones used by the Air Force. Ethan Miller/Getty Images

program saw the pilot removed from the battlefield, as UAVs could be remotely operated from thousands of miles away. The F-35 Joint Strike Fighter promised to be a terrifically versatile multirole fighter package, although its cost was many times that of the F-15 and F-16.

The United States Air Force continued to maintain two legs of the Pentagon's nuclear "triad," with its intercontinental ballistic missile force and its strategic bomber fleet falling under its Global Strike Command. The Air Force also expanded its influence into cyberspace in 2009 with the creation of the 24th Air Force, which was tasked with providing network security for United States Air Force and Department of Defense operations worldwide.

CONCLUSION

In the century since the dawn of powered flight, air forces have evolved from novelties to necessities, as even the smallest nations can boast some form of aerial defense network. From the wood and canvas biplanes of World War I to the stealthy jets of the 21st century, military aircraft continue to evoke fascination and wonder, as evidenced by the popularity of air shows around the world. In spite of such crowd-pleasing civilian endeavors, air forces remain first and foremost an element of an integrated defense strategy. The U.S. island-hopping campaign in the Pacific in World War II was dictated partially by the need to acquire air bases that were within striking distance of Japan. A generation later, in-air refuelling techniques allowed long-range bombers to strike targets on the other side of the world. In the 21st century, advances in electronics and satellite communication allowed pilots to leave the battlefield entirely, guiding UAVs with the flick of a joystick. The ability of militaries to project force by air has increased exponentially over time, and it has fundamentally transformed the way wars are fought.

GLOSSARY

airlift A system of transporting cargo or passengers by aircraft often to or from an otherwise inaccessible area.

astronautics The science of the construction and operation of vehicles for travel in space beyond Earth's atmosphere.

avionics The development and production of electronic instruments for use in aviation and astronautics; also, the instruments themselves.

ballast A heavy substance placed in such a way as to improve stability and control (as of the draft of a ship or the buoyancy of a balloon).

blitzkrieg A violent surprise offensive by massed air forces and mechanized ground forces in close coordination.

court-martial A court for people in the military who are accused of breaking military law.

cyberespionage The practice of obtaining sensitive information without the owner's permission from computers or digital transmissions and communications for the purposes of gaining competitive advantage or for intelligence gathering.

dogfight A fight between two or more fighter planes, usually at close quarters.

fly-by-wire Of, relating to, being, or utilizing a flight-control system in which controls are operated electrically rather than mechanically.

flying ace A pilot who has shot down five or more enemy aircraft.

flying circus A rotary echelon formation of airplanes in action.

force projection A country's ability to conduct military operations outside of its own borders.

garrison A military post.

guerrilla Of or relating to an irregular military force fighting small-scale, limited actions, in concert with an overall political-military strategy, against conventional military forces.

hard power The use of coercion and often military power in international relations.

interrupter gear A device attached to
military aircraft that allows a gun to fire
without damaging the propeller.

kamikaze A member of a Japanese air-
attack corps in World War II assigned
to make a suicidal crash on a target (as a
ship).

Mach number A number representing
the ratio of the speed of a body (as an
aircraft) to the speed of sound in a sur-
rounding medium (as air).

matériel Equipment, apparatus, and
supplies used by an organization or
institution.

no-fly zone An area over which military aircraft are not permitted to fly, especially
during a conflict.

ordnance Military supplies, including weapons, ammunition, combat vehicles, and
maintenance tools and equipment.

payload The load carried by a vehicle exclu-
sive of what is necessary for its operation.

reconnaissance Of or relating to an explor-
atory military survey of enemy territory.

shock and awe A military strategy in which
one side uses considerable power against
the other, especially during the initial
stages of a conflict, in order to achieve

early dominance over the enemy.

soft power The use of persuasion, often through economic or cultural influence, as opposed to coercion, in international relations.

sortie A sudden issuing of troops from a defensive position against the enemy.

supersonic Of, being, or relating to speeds from one to five times the speed of sound in air.

workhorse A dependable machine or vehicle that is used to do a lot of work.

FOR MORE INFORMATION

Air Force Historical Foundation (AFHF)
P.O. Box 790
Clinton, MD 20735-0790
(301) 736-1959
Web site: http://www.afhistoricalfoundation
.org
The AFHF is a nonprofit organization that
promotes the preservation and apprecia-
tion of the history of the United States
Air Force. It provides historical information on policies and air- and space-related
actions of the United States Air Force to
help inform policy-making and public
opinion. To that end, it publishes the semi-
annual *Air Power History* journal.

Canadian War Museum
1 Vimy Place
Ottawa, ON K1A 0M8
Canada
(800) 555-5621

Web site: http://www.warmuseum.ca

Through exhibitions featuring art, artifacts, and memoirs, as well as interactive presentations, the Canadian War Museum engages visitors with the history of the Canadian military from its inception to the present. It also offers a variety of educational programs on the history of the Canadian armed forces.

Directorate of History and Heritage (DHH)
National Defence Headquarters
101 Colonel By Drive
Ottawa, ON K1A 0K2
Canada
(613) 998-7058
Web site: http://www.cmp-cpm.forces.gc.ca/dhh-dhp/index-eng.asp

The DHH is an organization under the Canadian Department of National Defence dating back to the First World War. Its museum system and publications offer a wealth of information on the history of the Canadian Forces for researchers and the general public.

Eighth Air Force Historical Society (8thAFHS)
P.O. Box 956
Pooler, GA 31322

(912) 748-8884

Web site: http://www.8thafhs.org

Associated with the Mighty Eighth Air
Force Heritage Museum in Savannah,
Georgia, the 8thAFHS works to promote
the heritage of the famous U.S. Eighth
Air Force stationed in England during
World War II. Through newsletters,
chapter meetings, and correspondence
with foreign societies, the 8thAFHS
preserves the accomplishments of an
important command of the United States
Air Force, which continues to fight to
this day.

National Museum of the U.S. Air Force

1100 Spaatz Street

Wright-Patterson Air Force Base

Dayton, OH 45433

(937) 255-3286

Web site: http://www.nationalmuseum.af.mil

The National Museum of the U.S. Air
Force hosts galleries of artifacts and
exhibits—including displays of aircraft,
engines, and weapons—from the United
States Air Force's inception through
the present. Among the services that
the museum provides are educational
programs for students on the Air Force

and armed conflicts in which the United
States has participated.

Smithsonian National Air and Space Museum
Independence Ave at 6th Street SW
Washington, DC 20560
(202) 633-1000
Web site: http://airandspace.si.edu
The Smithsonian National Air and Space
    Museum contains the world's largest col-
    lection of aviation- and space-related
    artifacts. Having obtained the first pieces
    of its collection in 1896, the National Air
    and Space Museum has grown into one of
    the largest aeronautic and space research
    facilities in the world, with priceless exhib-
    its, resources, and publications for scholars,
    educators, and the public alike.

WEB SITES

Due to the changing nature of Internet
    links, Rosen Educational Services has
    developed an online list of Web sites
    related to the subject of this book. This
    site is updated regularly. Please use this
    link to access the list:

http://www.rosenlinks.com/armed/airfor

FOR FURTHER READING

Dolan, Edward F. *Careers in the U.S. Air Force.* New York, NY: Benchmark Books, 2009.

Freedman, Jeri. *Your Career in the Air Force.* New York, NY: Rosen, 2011.

Gregory, Josh. *Aircraft Pilot.* North Mankato, MN: Cherry Lake, 2012.

Gregory, Josh. *Avionics Technician.* North Mankato, MN: Cherry Lake, 2012.

Masters, Nancy Robinson. *Drone Pilot.* North Mankato, MN: Cherry Lake, 2012.

Masters, Nancy Robinson. *Pararescue Jumper.* North Mankato, MN: Cherry Lake, 2012.

Nardo, Don. *Special Operations: Search and Rescue.* Greensboro, NC: Morgan Reynolds, 2012.

Porterfield, Jason. *USAF Special Tactics Teams.* New York, NY: Rosen Central, 2008.

Ryan, Peter. *Black Ops and Other Special Missions of the U.S. Air Force Combat Control Team*. New York, NY: Rosen Central, 2012.

Vanderhoof, Gabrielle. *Air Force*. Broomall, PA: Mason Crest, 2010.

INDEX